A BEGINNER'S GUIDE TO
SKIRTS

Learn how to make **24** different skirts from 8 basic shapes

WENDY WARD

CICO BOOKS
LONDON NEW YORK

The measurements in this book are given in both imperial and metric. Please follow one system throughout and do not mix the two.

Published in 2016 by CICO Books
An imprint of Ryland Peters & Small Ltd

20–21 Jockey's Fields   341 E 116th St
London WC1R 4BW   New York, NY 10029

www.rylandpeters.com

10 9 8 7 6 5 4 3

A CIP catalog record for this book is available from the Library of Congress and the British Library.

ISBN: 978 1 78249 370 9

Printed in China

Editor: Sarah Hoggett
Designer: Geoff Borin
Additional design: Alison Fenton
Photographer: Julian Ward
Illustrator: Wendy Ward
Stylist: Rob Merrett

In-house editor: Anna Galkina
Art director: Sally Powell
Production controller: David Hearn
Publishing manager: Penny Craig
Publisher: Cindy Richards

CONTENTS

INTRODUCTION

A skirt is one of the easiest garments to make for yourself and the easiest to fit. I have been teaching people how to sew since 2007 and a skirt is usually my recommendation for a first dressmaking project. This book contains eight basic skirt projects that I have designed to suit all levels of sewing ability and tastes, from an easy pull-on jersey pencil skirt to a full-on feminine bubble skirt.

I am a firm believer in making everyday clothing, a wardrobe of core basics that fit you well, that are comfortable, that suit you, and that you wear again and again.

In this book I show you how you can adapt the basic patterns by adding seams and pleats, by color blocking and mixing fabrics, by adding topstitching and pockets. The devil is in the detail and I'll show you how to perfect those details. I won't be showing you shortcuts, but the "Wendy way" of doing things —my way, that I've developed and perfected through years of sewing for myself, for others, and through teaching others to sew. My students will tell you that I'm a stickler for doing things right and taking the time needed to get the best results. If you start off on your sewing journey being slapdash and without paying attention to detail, you'll struggle to achieve it later on down the line; but if you start off doing it right and trying your best, you'll always work that way and speediness will come with practice.

Here are some great examples:

Assuntina started coming to my sewing classes in 2014 and was really nervous: nervous about joining a group class and nervous about her perceived lack of ability. She started off with some cushions, then she embellished them with some appliqué and embroidery, then she made an A-line skirt that she was amazed fitted her and that she enjoyed wearing. Then there was no stopping her; she regularly comes to class wearing her latest make, demanding to have her photo taken!

Debbie was inspired in 2013 by the first series of *The Great British Sewing Bee* on television to have a go at sewing. She'd never done it before and didn't have a sewing machine, but wanted to try because she's much taller than most average ready-to-wear clothing is made for and was stuck with limited choices when out clothes shopping. The first thing she made was an apron; the cutting was a bit wobbly, the stitching was a bit wobbly, but she did it, loved it, and still uses it. She now regularly wears clothes she's made, from smart dresses for her job in sales to pajamas and yoga pants, and every time I see her she's making something for someone else now, too.

So you're in safe hands—just have a try and see what happens. There are many reasons to start sewing: to make clothes that fit, as a hobby/creative outlet, to meet like-minded people, to make clothes you want to wear from good-quality fabric, and to be able to know where your clothes and fabric came from. In these days of globalization and the damage done to the environment and people by the textile and clothing industry, it's good to be able to play a small part. I'm passionate about changing these unethical systems and the part that sustainable fashion can play. Making your own clothes can bring about a new love of and appreciation for how and where clothes are made. The multi-colored knee-length sample of the Fallowfield Pencil Skirt (page 78) has been made from organic cotton denim, is hand dyed, and is one-of-a-kind.

If you need any more convincing of the joy of sewing, it's also good for you! If you need some moral support, why not take this book along to your local sewing class or meet up with a few friends and sew together? Try and get a little sewing station set up at home so that your sewing machine and current project are always on hand and quick to work on. Even just 15 minutes a day will eventually yield wonderful results. Treat sewing time as "you time" and a pleasurable thing to do.

I hope you enjoy your journey. You can share in a bit of mine with the story behind the names of the projects; they're named chronologically after places that have been significant during my career so far.

HOW TO USE THIS BOOK

- The projects are presented in the book in order of difficulty, so if you are a complete beginner start with the Roewood Jersey Pencil Skirt and work your way through; if you're a more experienced dressmaker, you can dive into whichever project takes your fancy!

- Each of the eight projects has three different versions. The most basic version of each project is shown made up in denim and is the easiest one to start with.

- All the skirts are designed to sit on the natural waistline. I find this the most comfortable place for skirts to sit, as it is usually the narrowest part of your body and so is the natural place for a garment to sit. If you prefer to wear skirts lower on the waist, see Fitting, page 155.

- Fabric advice is given with each project, so refer to the What Fabric Should I Use? section in each project introduction. There is also a Fabric Glossary at the back of the book (page 157) to help you decide whether or not a fabric will be right for your project.

- Imperial and metric measurement systems are used throughout the book. Choose one system and stick with it throughout the making of a project.

- Read the Sizing & Taking Measurements section (page 130) thoroughly before starting any of the projects and take your measurements accurately. You want to make clothes that fit!

- Before you start a project, read the You Will Need list to see what fabric and other things like zippers are required.

- The techniques needed for each project are noted in the introduction to each project, so read through these techniques before you start to sew your skirt.

- Full-size paper patterns for all of the projects are on pull-out pattern sheets inside the front and back cover of the book. Instructions for how to use them are given in Using Paper Patterns, page 131.

- There are detailed cutting plans in each project's instructions. To work out which one to follow, refer to the chart in the You Will Need list for the version you're making.

- Seam allowances are given at the start of the instructions for each project. All seam allowances are included in the patterns.

- Read through all the instructions carefully before you start to make sure you're following only the steps relevant to the version of the skirt that you're making (each skirt has three versions).

ROEWOOD—THE JERSEY PENCIL SKIRT

A stretchy pencil skirt is the best kind of skirt—comfy but stylish. This is a great introduction to working with knitted fabrics and an ideal project for beginners, as it's simple to fit and quick and easy to make. You can whip up a collection of the basic plain version in the short length in lightweight jersey for summer vacations.

My black-and-gold version is a great solution for a dressy skirt. And when you've mastered basic seams, have a go at the gathered-side version for something a little different.

FINISHED SKIRT MEASUREMENTS

Size (Your actual hip measurement)

	34¾ in. (88 cm)	36¼ in. (92 cm)	38 in. (96 cm)	39½ in. (100 cm)	41 in. (104 cm)	43 in. (109 cm)	45 in. (114 cm)	47 in. (119 cm)	49 in. (124 cm)	51 in. (129 cm)
Waist (before elastic is added)	26¾ in. (68 cm)	28½ in. (72 cm)	30 in. (76 cm)	31½ in. (80 cm)	33 in. (84 cm)	35 in. (89 cm)	37 in. (94 cm)	39 in. (99 cm)	41 in. (104 cm)	43 in. (109 cm)
Hips	31½ in. (80 cm)	33 in. (84 cm)	34½ in. (88 cm)	36¼ in. (92 cm)	38 in. (96 cm)	40 in. (101 cm)	42 in. (106 cm)	43¾ in. (111 cm)	45½ in. (116 cm)	47½ in. (121 cm)
Length (short)	17¼ in. (44 cm)	17½ in. (44.5 cm)	17¾ in. (45 cm)	18 in. (45.5 cm)	18¼ in. (46 cm)	18⅜ in. (46.5 cm)	18½ in. (47 cm)	18¾ in. (47.5 cm)	19 in. (48 cm)	19 in. (48.5 cm)
Length (full)	27¾ in. (70.5 cm)	28 in. (71.5 cm)	28½ in. (72.5 cm)	29 in. (73.5 cm)	29½ in. (74.5 cm)	29¾ in. (75.5 cm)	30 in. (76.5 cm)	30½ in. (77.5 cm)	31 in. (78.5 cm)	31¼ in. (79.5 cm)

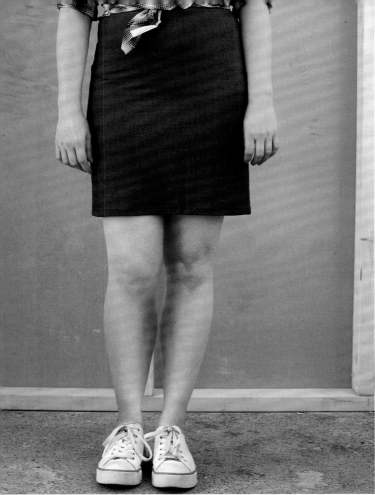

You will notice that the waist measurement is just over 1½ in. (4 cm) bigger than the actual waist measurement given for each size; this is because it is fitted to your exact waist size when you add the elastic. Also, the skirt hip measurement is 3 in. (8 cm) smaller than the actual hip measurement; this is to allow the fabric to stretch for a snug fit. This is called "negative ease" (see page 130).

Follow the instructions in Sizing & Taking Measurements (page 130) for exactly where and how to measure yourself and how to choose which size to make.

WHAT FABRIC SHOULD I USE?

This skirt must be made in a knit fabric, ideally with at least 3% elastane/spandex. This is so that the skirt will stretch, but will also recover again, meaning that it won't develop a saggy bottom over time! Single jersey and Ponte Roma work best, but you could try it in a loopback sweatshirt (or French terry) for a casual sporty skirt, or a sweater knit fabric for a snuggly

winter maxi skirt in the longer length.

The skirt works well in solid colors, prints, or stripes and the paneled version is perfect for mixing colors and/or prints.

My samples are made in the following fabrics:

• Plain denim jersey short version: polyester/elastane single jersey (above left)

• Black-and-gold paneled version: the black fabric is viscose/elastane Ponte Roma; the gold fabric is stretch metallic PVC (above right)

• Gathered burgundy version: viscose/elastane Ponte Roma (opposite)

If you are unsure whether a fabric is suitable, check the Fabrics Glossary (page 157).

YOU WILL NEED

For all versions

Matching sewing thread

Elastic 1¼ in. (3 cm) wide—enough to comfortably fit your waist plus 1¼ in. (3 cm)

For side-gathered version

½ in. (1 cm) wide elastic to make gathered sides:
size 34¾ in. (88 cm) hip—15 in. (37 cm)
size 36¼ in. (92 cm) hip—15¼ in. (38 cm)
size 38 in. (96 cm) hip—15½ in. (39 cm)
size 39½ in. (100 cm) hip—15¾ in. (40 cm)
size 41 in. (104 cm) hip—16 in. (41 cm)
size 43 in. (109 cm) hip—16½ in. (42 cm)
size 45 in. (114 cm) hip—17 in. (43 cm)
size 47 in. (119 cm) hip—17½ in. (44 cm)
size 49 in. (124 cm) hip—17¾ in. (45 cm)
size 51 in. (129 cm) hip—18 in. (46 cm)

Roewood plain, short version

FABRIC REQUIREMENTS

Size (Your actual hip measurement)

Fabric width	34¾ in. (88 cm)	36¼ in. (92 cm)	38 in. (96 cm)	39½ in. (100 cm)	41 in. (104 cm)	43 in. (109 cm)	45 in. (114 cm)	47 in. (119 cm)	49 in. (124 cm)	51 in. (129 cm)
44 in. (112 cm) or wider	⅝ yd (0.6 m)	⅝ yd (0.6 m)	⅝ yd (0.6 m)	⅝ yd (0.6 m)	⅝ yd (0.6 m)	⅝ yd (0.6 m)	⅝ yd (0.6 m)	1⅜ yd (1.2 m)	1⅜ yd (1.2 m)	1⅜ yd (1.2 m)
55 in. (140 cm) or wider	⅝ yd (0.6 m)	⅝ yd (0.6 m)	⅝ yd (0.6 m)	⅝ yd (0.6 m)	⅝ yd (0.6 m)	⅝ yd (0.6 m)	⅝ yd (0.6 m)	⅝ yd (0.6 m)	⅝ yd (0.6 m)	⅝ yd (0.6 m)

WHICH CUTTING PLAN TO FOLLOW

Fabric width	34¾ in. (88 cm)	36¼ in. (92 cm)	38 in. (96 cm)	39½ in. (100 cm)	41 in. (104 cm)	43 in. (109 cm)	45 in. (114 cm)	47 in. (119 cm)	49 in. (124 cm)	51 in. (129 cm)
44 in. (112 cm) or wider	1	1	1	1	1	1	1	2	2	2
55 in. (140 cm) or wider	1	1	1	1	1	1	1	1	1	1

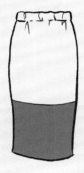

Roewood paneled version

FABRIC REQUIREMENTS

Size (Your actual hip measurement)

	34¾ in. (88 cm)	36¼ in. (92 cm)	38 in. (96 cm)	39½ in. (100 cm)	41 in. (104 cm)	43 in. (109 cm)	45 in. (114 cm)	47 in. (119 cm)	49 in. (124 cm)	51 in. (129 cm)
Main / upper fabric										
Fabric width 44 in. (112 cm) or wider	⅝ yd (0.6 m)	⅝ yd (0.6 m)	⅝ yd (0.6 m)	⅝ yd (0.6 m)	⅝ yd (0.6 m)	⅝ yd (0.6 m)	⅝ yd (0.6 m)	1⅜ yd (1.2 m)	1⅜ yd (1.2 m)	1⅜ yd (1.2 m)
55 in. (140 cm) or wider	⅝ yd (0.6 m)	⅝ yd (0.6 m)	⅝ yd (0.6 m)	⅝ yd (0.6 m)	⅝ yd (0.6 m)	⅝ yd (0.6 m)	⅝ yd (0.6 m)	⅝ yd (0.6 m)	⅝ yd (0.6 m)	⅝ yd (0.6 m)
Lower panel fabric										
44 in. (112 cm) or wider	½ yd (0.4 m)	½ yd (0.4 m)	½ yd (0.4 m)	½ yd (0.4 m)	½ yd (0.4 m)	½ yd (0.4 m)	½ yd (0.4 m)	⅝ yd (0.8 m)	⅝ yd (0.8 m)	⅝ yd (0.8 m)
55 in. (140 cm) or wider	½ yd (0.4 m)	½ yd (0.4 m)	½ yd (0.4 m)	½ yd (0.4 m)	½ yd (0.4 m)	½ yd (0.4 m)	½ yd (0.4 m)	½ yd (0.4 m)	½ yd (0.4 m)	½ yd (0.4 m)

WHICH CUTTING PLAN TO FOLLOW

	34¾ in. (88 cm)	36¼ in. (92 cm)	38 in. (96 cm)	39½ in. (100 cm)	41 in. (104 cm)	43 in. (109 cm)	45 in. (114 cm)	47 in. (119 cm)	49 in. (124 cm)	51 in. (129 cm)
Main / upper fabric										
Fabric width 44 in. (112 cm) or wider	1	1	1	1	1	1	1	2	2	2
55 in. (140 cm) or wider	1	1	1	1	1	1	1	1	1	1
Lower panel fabric										
44 in. (112 cm) or wider	3	3	3	3	3	3	3	4	4	4
55 in. (140 cm) or wider	3	3	3	3	3	3	3	3	3	3

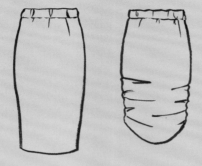

Roewood long plain or side-gathered version

FABRIC REQUIREMENTS

Size (Your actual hip measurement)

Fabric width	34¾ in. (88 cm)	36¼ in. (92 cm)	38 in. (96 cm)	39½ in. (100 cm)	41 in. (104 cm)	43 in. (109 cm)	45 in. (114 cm)	47 in. (119 cm)	49 in. (124 cm)	51 in. (129 cm)
44 in. (112 cm) or wider	1 yd (0.9 m)	1 yd (0.9 m)	1 yd (0.9 m)	1 yd (0.9 m)	1 yd (0.9 m)	1 yd (0.9 m)	1 yd (0.9 m)	2 yd (1.7 m)	2 yd (1.7 m)	2 yd (1.7 m)
55 in. (140 cm) or wider	1 yd (0.9 m)	1 yd (0.9 m)	1 yd (0.9 m)	1 yd (0.9 m)	1 yd (0.9 m)	1 yd (0.9 m)	1 yd (0.9 m)	1 yd (0.9 m)	1 yd (0.9 m)	1 yd (0.9 m)
Elastic ½ in. (1 cm) wide for side-gathered version	15 in. (37 cm)	15¼ in. (38 cm)	15½ in. (39 cm)	15¾ in. (40 cm)	16 in. (41 cm)	16½ in. (42 cm)	17 in. (43 cm)	17½ in. (44 cm)	17¾ in. (45 cm)	18 in. (46 cm)

WHICH CUTTING PLAN TO FOLLOW

Fabric width	34¾ in. (88 cm)	36¼ in. (92 cm)	38 in. (96 cm)	39½ in. (100 cm)	41 in. (104 cm)	43 in. (109 cm)	45 in. (114 cm)	47 in. (119 cm)	49 in. (124 cm)	51 in. (129 cm)
44 in. (112 cm) or wider	1	1	1	1	1	1	1	2	2	2
55 in. (140 cm) or wider	1	1	1	1	1	1	1	1	1	1

PREPARING YOUR PATTERN PIECES

Trace off the pattern pieces in the size you need from the pattern sheet—skirt front and skirt back (in short or full length), waistband, and lower panel (if required. Note: on the pattern sheets, the lower panel starts from the point the short version ends, the bottom of the panel is at the same point as the bottom of the long version). Read the instructions in Using Paper Patterns, page 131.

CUTTING YOUR FABRIC

Make sure you read the Fabrics section (page 132) before you lay out your pattern pieces and take the scissors to your fabric!

Following the cutting plan for your fabric width, pin the pattern pieces to the fabric and cut out. Transfer any markings to the fabric (see page 133).

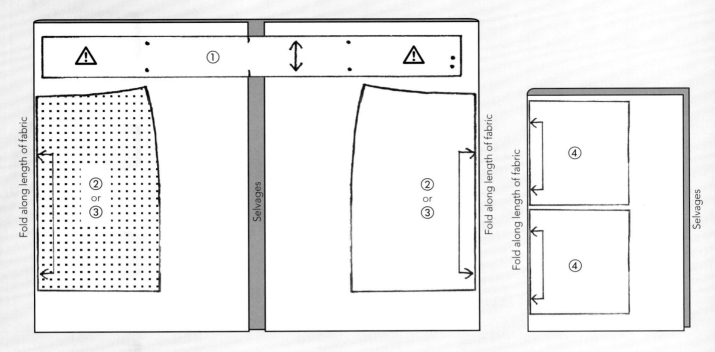

Cutting plan 1 and 3 (above)

Cutting plan 2 and 4 (below)

Pattern pieces

① Waistband

② Skirt front and back (short)

③ Skirt front and back (long)

④ Lower panel front and back

Key

Fabric

Right side   Wrong side

Pattern pieces

Printed side up   Printed side down

⚠ Cut out this pattern piece from the fabric unfolded once all the other pattern pieces have been cut

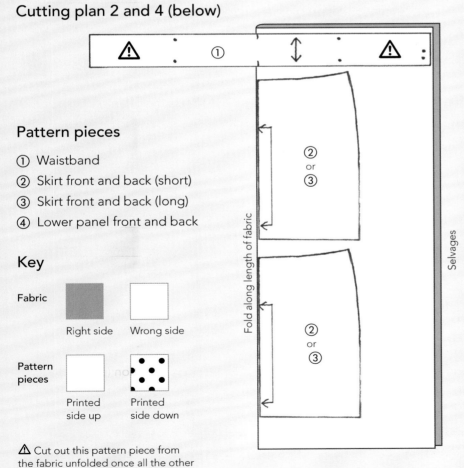

PUTTING IT TOGETHER

Seam allowance is ⅝ in. (1.5 cm)

Hem allowance is ¾ in. (2 cm)

Key to diagrams

Right side   Wrong side   Interfacing

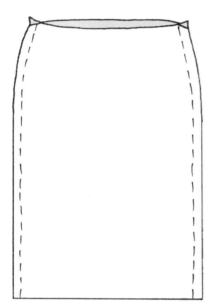

All versions: joining the side seams

Place the skirt front and back right sides together and pin the side seams. Start pinning at each end of the seam first and work your way toward the center so that the edges can't stretch. Baste (tack) and machine (see Sewing Knitted Fabrics—Seams, page 134.) Press the seams either open or to one side, depending on which stitch you have used.

Paneled version

1 Join the side seams of the lower panels of the skirt in the same way as those for the main (upper) fabric.

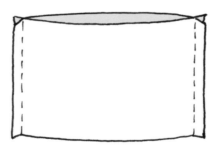

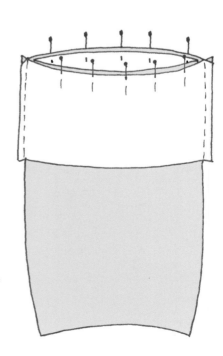

2 Turn the main fabric skirt right side out, but leave the lower panel inside out. With right sides together, place the lower panel over the hem of the main skirt, with the top edge of the lower panel along the bottom edge of the main skirt. Line up the side seams, center fronts, and center backs, and pin the panel seam together. Baste if necessary, then machine (see Sewing Knitted Fabrics—Seams, page 134). Press the seam either open or to one side, depending on which stitch you have used.

All versions: attaching the waistband

1 Fold the waistband in half widthwise, right sides together, pin the short ends together. Machine, using a stretch straight stitch (see Sewing Knitted Fabrics—Seams, page 134), making sure you leave a gap between the dots; you'll be threading your elastic through this gap in the seam later.

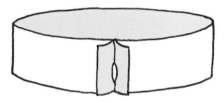

2 Press the seam open.

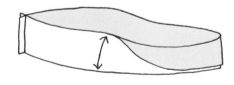

3 Fold the waistband in half lengthwise, wrong sides together, aligning the two raw edges.

4 Press the fold to keep it in place, pin the raw edges together and mark the center front and side seams with pins. Baste the raw edges together.

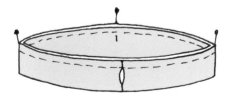

5 With the skirt right side out, slide the waistband over the waist edge of the skirt, aligning the raw edges of the waistband with the raw edge at the top of the skirt. Make sure you can see the gap in the center back seam of the waistband and it isn't on the underside of the waistband touching the skirt so that, when you flip the waistband up once it's attached, the opening will be on the inside of the skirt. Pin the waistband to the skirt, matching the pins marking the waistband center front and side seams with the center front and side seams of the skirt, and the waistband center back seam with the center back of the skirt.

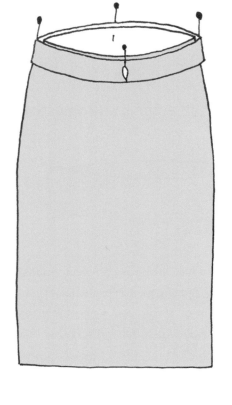

6 Baste and machine (see Sewing Knitted Fabrics— Seams, page 134).

TIP

Be careful to keep this seam allowance really accurate or your elastic won't fit in the waistband.

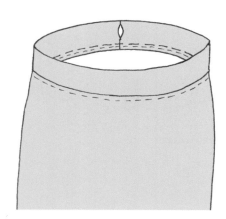

7 Press the seam toward the skirt and topstitch it in place using a stretch straight stitch (see Sewing Knitted Fabrics—Seams, page 134).

8 Cut a piece of wide elastic long enough to fit comfortably around your waist plus 1¼ in. (3 cm). Insert the elastic into the waistband (see Using Elastic—Elasticated Waistbands, page 141).

Gathered-sides version

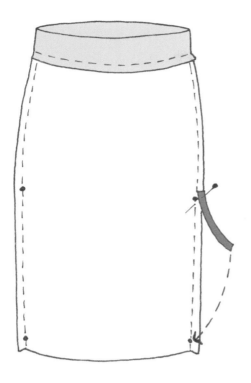

Turn the skirt inside out. Cut the narrow elastic into two equal-sized pieces. Pin one end of one piece of elastic to the dot marked on the side seam, stretching the elastic until it reaches the other elastic placement dot, and sew it onto the seam (see Using Elastic to Add Gathers, page 142). Attach the other length of elastic to the other side seam in the same way.

All versions: hem

Fold over a ¾-in. (2-cm) hem allowance to the wrong side, pin in place, and hem (see Sewing Knitted Fabrics—Hems, page 134). For the gathered-sides version, the hem should cover the bottom of the elastic.

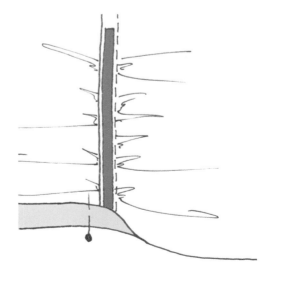

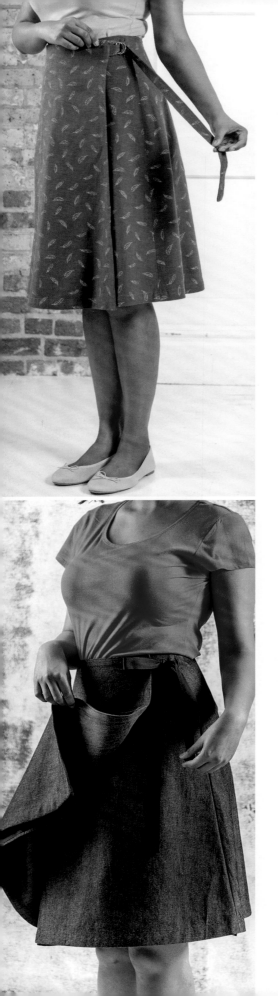

GRANVILLE—THE WRAP SKIRT

A wrap skirt is the perfect first skirt project—no zippers to worry about, forgiving on the fit, and a great place to have your first attempt at an easy patch pocket.

This wrap skirt is a flattering and comfortable A-line shape that works in a wide variety of fabrics. In a lightweight denim, it makes a gorgeous casual skirt that can be worn with flip-flops in summer or with tights and sneakers in the colder months. Its simple shape makes it the perfect skirt to show off a fabulous print and a printed cotton or linen would make an ideal skirt to throw on over a swimsuit or bikini—a slightly more sophisticated alternative to a sarong! Playing around with the width of the ties can also create different looks: imagine a drapey, silk-crepe version with luxurious wide ties fastened in a bow. You could even mix and match fabrics by making each part of the skirt in a different fabric.

The worry with a wrap skirt is often a "wardrobe malfunction" involving the wrap blowing open. Don't worry, you've got it covered in this skirt: the front is doubled up to make the wrap, so there's no danger of doing a Marilyn in a gust of wind. You'll even stay prim and proper when seated.

For such a seemingly simple skirt, there really are lots of different ways to make it. There are three different lengths, and it can be fastened with self-fabric ties, bought ties, buttons, or simple D-rings. The inside of the skirt can be finished either with a facing or completely lined, which then makes the skirt reversible.

Start with a completely plain version with bought cotton tape for the ties and move on to adding pockets and a reversible lined version as you gain confidence. It's also a good skirt to practice your first buttonholes, as there are only two of them—and if you really don't want to brave it with a button, you can always use a sew-on popper snap instead.

Follow the instructions in Sizing & Taking Measurements (page 130) for exactly where and how to measure yourself and how to choose which size to make.

The tie fastening is tidy and neat, but just in case it's not obvious, here is how to fasten it!
• Wrap the long tie attached to the left/under front skirt around your waist completely and feed it back through the opening in the left side seam.
• Fasten the long tie to the short tie attached to the right/upper front skirt.
• Adjust the tightness of the ties to your own comfort.

WITH THIS SKIRT, YOU WILL PRACTICE THE FOLLOWING BASIC TECHNIQUES:

- Seams

- Hems

- Attaching facings

- Patch pockets

- Buttons and buttonholes (or sew-on popper snaps for the faint hearted!)

FINISHED SKIRT MEASUREMENTS

Size (Your actual hip measurement)

	34¾ in. (88 cm)	36¼ in. (92 cm)	38 in. (96 cm)	39½ in. (100 cm)	41 in. (104 cm)	43 in. (109 cm)	45 in. (114 cm)	47 in. (119 cm)	49 in. (124 cm)	51 in. (129 cm)
Waist*	25½ in. (65 cm)	27 in. (69 cm)	28¾ in. (73 cm)	30¼ in. (77 cm)	32 in. (81 cm)	34 in. (86 cm)	36 in. (91 cm)	38 in. (96 cm)	40 in. (101 cm)	42 in. (106 cm)
Hips	38 in. (96 cm)	40 in. (101 cm)	41½ in. (105 cm)	43 in. (109 cm)	44½ in. (113 cm)	46½ in. (118 cm)	48½ in. (123 cm)	50½ in. (128 cm)	52½ in. (133 cm)	54½ in. (138 cm)
Approx. length from waist seam down center back (short version)	21 in. (53.5 cm)	21½ in. (54.5 cm)	22 in. (55.5 cm)	22¼ in. (56.5 cm)	22¾ in. (57.5 cm)	23 in. (58.5 cm)	23½ in. (59.5 cm)	24 in. (60.5 cm)	24¼ in. (61.5 cm)	24¾ in. (62.5 cm)
Approx. length from waist seam down center back (knee-length version)	22¾ in. (57.5 cm)	23 in. (58.5 cm)	23½ in. (59.5 cm)	24 in. (60.5 cm)	24¼ in. (61.5 cm)	24¾ in. (62.5 cm)	25 in. (63.5 cm)	25½ in. (64.5 cm)	25¾ in. (65.5 cm)	26¼ in. (66.5 cm)
Approx. length from waist seam down center back (long version)	24½ in. (61.5 cm)	24¾ in. (62.5 in.)	25 in. (63.5 cm)	25½ in. (64.5 cm)	25¾ in. (65.5 cm)	26¼ in. (66.5 cm)	26½ in. (67.5 cm)	27 in. (68.5 cm)	27½ in. (69.5 cm)	27¾ in. (70.5 cm)

* As this style is a wrap skirt there is some leeway in this measurement, as it depends how tight or loose you choose to fasten the skirt.

WHAT FABRIC SHOULD I USE?

The wrap skirt looks great (and is easiest to sew) in medium-weight woven fabrics such as denims, linen, cotton/linen blends, corduroy, cotton chintz, cotton poplin, and lightweight wools. It's best to avoid fabrics with elastane as the skirt does not have a fixed waistband—you don't want the waist of the skirt to stretch out of shape. It will work well in either solid colors or prints.

It could be made in almost any other woven fabric, but don't choose a knitted fabric.

My samples are made in the following fabrics:

• Knee-length denim version with patch pocket: cotton denim and cotton herringbone tape ties

• Long feather print version with D-ring fastening: linen

• Short African wax print version with button fastening: cotton

If you are unsure whether a fabric is suitable, check the Fabrics Glossary (page 157).

This pattern is suitable for one-way prints and fabrics with a surface texture or pile.

YOU WILL NEED

For all versions

Matching sewing thread

For tie versions (including D-rings)

If you don't want to make the ties from your fabric, you will need approx. 70 in. (1.75 m) cotton herringbone tape, 1 in. (2.5 cm) wide for the simple tie version, or 24 in. (61 cm) for the D-ring version

For button fastening version

2 x buttons approx. ¾–1¼ in. (2–3 cm) in diameter (or 2 x sew-on popper snaps if you prefer)

For D-ring version

1 set of D-rings, 1–1¼ in. (2.5–3 cm) wide

For faced version

2¾ yd (2.5 m) bias binding (optional)

Granville short version with facing and button fastening

FABRIC REQUIREMENTS

Size (Your actual hip measurement)

Fabric width	34¾ in. (88 cm)	36¼ in. (92 cm)	38 in. (96 cm)	39½ in. (100 cm)	41 in. (104 cm)	43 in. (109 cm)	45 in. (114 cm)	47 in. (119 cm)	49 in. (124 cm)	51 in. (129 cm)
44 in. (112 cm) or wider	2¾ yd (2.5 m)	2¾ yd (2.5 m)	2¾ yd (2.5 m)	2¾ yd (2.5 m)	2¾ yd (2.5 m)	2¾ yd (2.5 m)	2¾ yd (2.5 m)	2¾ yd (2.5 m)	2¾ yd (2.5 m)	2¾ yd (2.5 m)
55 in. (140 cm) or wider	2½ yd (2.3 m)	2½ yd (2.3 m)	2½ yd (2.3 m)	2½ yd (2.3 m)	2½ yd (2.3 m)	2½ yd (2.3 m)	2½ yd (2.3 m)	2½ yd (2.3 m)	2½ yd (2.3 m)	2½ yd (2.3 m)
Interfacing (36 in./90 cm wide)	1 yd (0.9 m)	1 yd (0.9 m)	1 yd (0.9 m)	1 yd (0.9 m)	1 yd (0.9 m)	1 yd (0.9 m)	1 yd (0.9 m)	1 yd (0.9 m)	1 yd (0.9 m)	1 yd (0.9 m)

WHICH CUTTING PLAN TO FOLLOW

Size (Your actual hip measurement)

	34¾ in. (88 cm)	36¼ in. (92 cm)	38 in. (96 cm)	39½ in. (100 cm)	41 in. (104 cm)	43 in. (109 cm)	45 in. (114 cm)	47 in. (119 cm)	49 in. (124 cm)	51 in. (129 cm)
44 in. (112 cm) or wider	1	1	1	1	1	1	1	1	1	1
55 in. (140 cm) or wider	2	2	2	2	2	2	2	2	2	2
Interfacing (36 in./90 cm wide)	3	3	3	3	3	3	3	3	3	3

Granville knee-length version with tape ties, lining, and contrast pocket

FABRIC REQUIREMENTS

Size (Your actual hip measurement)

	34¾ in. (88 cm)	36¼ in. (92 cm)	38 in. (96 cm)	39½ in. (100 cm)	41 in. (104 cm)	43 in. (109 cm)	45 in. (114 cm)	47 in. (119 cm)	49 in. (124 cm)	51 in. (129 cm)
Outer skirt										
Fabric width 44 in. (112 cm) or wider	2⅜ yd (2.1 m)	2⅜ yd (2.1 m)	2⅜ yd (2.1 m)	2⅜ yd (2.1 m)	2⅜ yd (2.1 m)	2⅜ yd (2.1 m)	2⅜ yd (2.1 m)	2⅜ yd (2.1 m)	2⅜ yd (2.1 m)	2⅜ yd (2.1 m)
55 in. (140 cm) or wider	2⅜ yd (2.1 m)	2⅜ yd (2.1 m)	2⅜ yd (2.1 m)	2⅜ yd (2.1 m)	2⅜ yd (2.1 m)	2⅜ yd (2.1 m)	2⅜ yd (2.1 m)	2⅜ yd (2.1 m)	2⅜ yd (2.1 m)	2⅜ yd (2.1 m)
Lining										
44 in. (112 cm) or wider	2¾ yd (2.5 m)	2¾ yd (2.5 m)	2¾ yd (2.5 m)	2¾ yd (2.5 m)	2¾ yd (2.5 m)	2¾ yd (2.5 m)	2¾ yd (2.5 m)	2¾ yd (2.5 m)	2¾ yd (2.5 m)	2¾ yd (2.5 m)
55 in. (140 cm) or wider	2½ yd (2.2 m)	2½ yd (2.2 m)	2½ yd (2.2 m)	2½ yd (2.2 m)	2½ yd (2.2 m)	2½ yd (2.2 m)	2½ yd (2.2 m)	2½ yd (2.2 m)	2½ yd (2.2 m)	2½ yd (2.2 m)

WHICH CUTTING PLAN TO FOLLOW

	34¾ in. (88 cm)	36¼ in. (92 cm)	38 in. (96 cm)	39½ in. (100 cm)	41 in. (104 cm)	43 in. (109 cm)	45 in. (114 cm)	47 in. (119 cm)	49 in. (124 cm)	51 in. (129 cm)
Outer										
44 in. (112 cm) or wider	4	4	4	4	4	4	4	4	4	4
55 in. (140 cm) or wider	6	6	6	6	6	6	6	6	6	6
Lining										
44 in. (112 cm) or wider	5	5	5	5	5	5	5	5	5	5
55 in. (140 cm) or wider	7	7	7	7	7	7	7	7	7	7

Granville long version with facing and D-ring fastening with fabric ties

FABRIC REQUIREMENTS

Size (Your actual hip measurement)

Fabric width	34¾ in. (88 cm)	36¼ in. (92 cm)	38 in. (96 cm)	39½ in. (100 cm)	41 in. (104 cm)	43 in. (109 cm)	45 in. (114 cm)	47 in. (119 cm)	49 in. (124 cm)	51 in. (129 cm)
44 in. (112 cm) or wider	3 yd (2.8 m)	3 yd (2.8 m)	3 yd (2.8 m)	3 yd (2.8 m)	3 yd (2.8 m)	3 yd (2.8 m)	3 yd (2.8 m)	3 yd (2.8 m)	3 yd (2.8 m)	3 yd (2.8 m)
55 in. (140 cm) or wider	3 yd (2.8 m)	3 yd (2.8 m)	3 yd (2.8 m)	3 yd (2.8 m)	3 yd (2.8 m)	3 yd (2.8 m)	3 yd (2.8 m)	3 yd (2.8 m)	3 yd (2.8 m)	3 yd (2.8 m)
Interfacing (36 in./90 cm wide)	40 in (1 m)	40 in (1 m)	40 in (1 m)	40 in (1 m)	40 in (1 m)	40 in (1 m)	40 in (1 m)	40 in (1 m)	40 in (1 m)	40 in (1 m)

WHICH CUTTING PLAN TO FOLLOW

Size (Your actual hip measurement)

	34¾ in. (88 cm)	36¼ in. (92 cm)	38 in. (96 cm)	39½ in. (100 cm)	41 in. (104 cm)	43 in. (109 cm)	45 in. (114 cm)	47 in. (119 cm)	49 in. (124 cm)	51 in. (129 cm)
44 in. (112 cm) or wider	8	8	8	8	8	8	8	8	8	8
55 in. (140 cm) or wider	8	8	8	8	8	8	8	8	8	8
Interfacing (36 in./90 cm wide)	3	3	3	3	3	3	3	3	3	3

PREPARING YOUR PATTERN PIECES

Trace off the pattern pieces in the size you need from the pattern sheet:

• Short version with facing and button fastening: skirt front, skirt back, back waist facing, front waist facing.

• Knee-length lined version with pocket: skirt front, skirt back, pocket band. Optional: long tie and short tie, or use purchased cotton herringbone tape for the ties.

• Long version with facing and D-ring fastening: skirt front, skirt back, back waist facing, front waist facing. Optional: short tie and D-ring tab, or use purchased cotton herringbone tape.

For all versions, you will need to cut out two (one pair of) fronts. Mark these as "left/under front" and "right/upper front" before you go any further on the wrong side of the fabric, or pin paper labels to them. The left and right refers to where they end up in the skirt when it's being worn; in other words, "left front" means the one that's against your left leg when you're wearing the skirt.

Read the instructions in Using Paper Patterns, page 131.

CUTTING YOUR FABRIC

Make sure you read the Fabrics section (page 132) before you lay out your pattern pieces and take the scissors to your fabric!

Following the cutting plan for your fabric width and garment size, pin the pattern pieces to the fabric and cut around carefully. Cut out all pieces in fabric; if you are making a version with facing, cut the front and back waist facing pieces in interfacing. Transfer any markings to the fabric (see page 133).

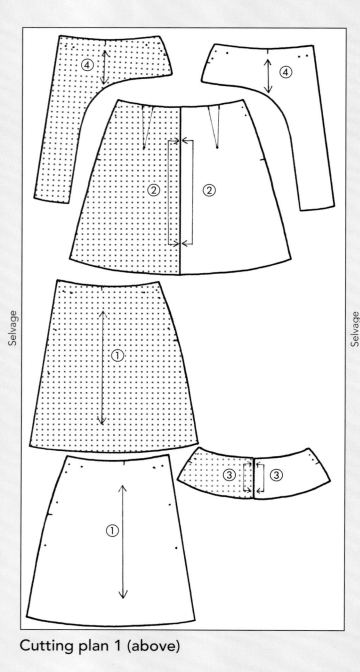

Cutting plan 1 (above)

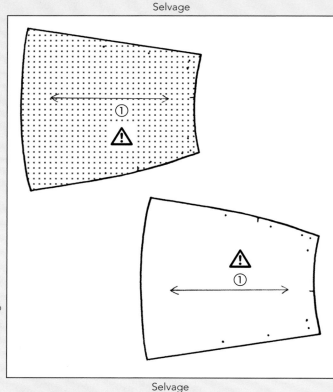
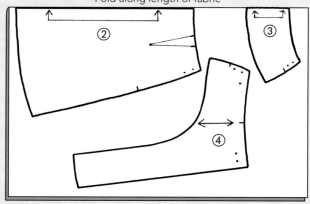

Cutting plan 2 (above)

⚠ Cut out these pattern pieces from the fabric unfolded once all the other pattern pieces have been cut

Pattern pieces

① Skirt front
② Skirt back
③ Back waist facing
④ Front facing
⑤ Pocket band
⑥ Short tie
⑦ Long tie

Key

Fabric

 Right side   Wrong side

Pattern pieces

 Printed side up   Printed side down

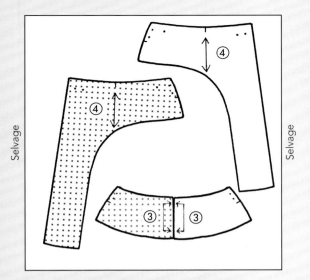

Cutting plan 3 (for interfacing)
(above)

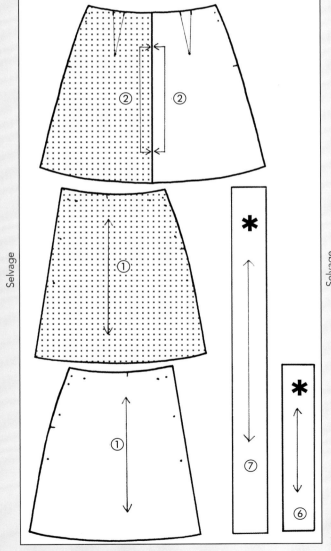

Cutting plan 4 (above)

Cutting plan 5 (above)

✱ The ties are optional: if you use herringbone tape
you don't need to cut them.

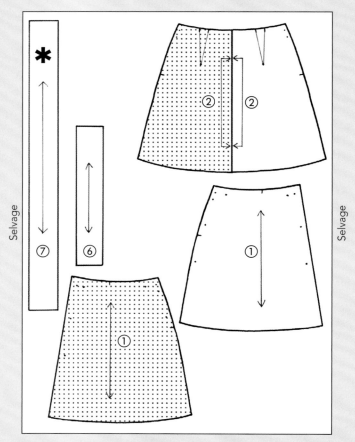

Cutting plan 6 (above)

* The ties are optional: if you use herringbone tape you don't need to cut them.

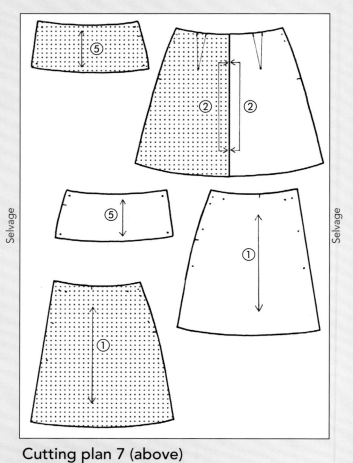

Cutting plan 7 (above)

Selvage

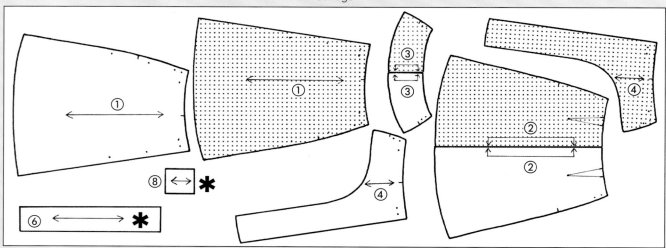

Cutting plan 8 (above) * The ties are optional: if you use herringbone tape you don't need to cut them.

Pattern pieces

① Skirt front
② Skirt back
③ Back waist facing
④ Front facing
⑤ Pocket band
⑥ Short tie
⑦ Long tie
⑧ D-ring tab

Key

Fabric

Right side

Wrong side

Pattern pieces

Printed side up

Printed side down

PUTTING IT TOGETHER

Seam allowance is ⅝ in. (1.5 cm)

Hem allowance is ¾ in. (2 cm)

Key to diagrams

Right side

Wrong side

Interfacing

All versions: stitching darts, staystitching, stitching side seams

1 Stitch the darts in the skirt back (see Darts, page 142).

2 Staystitch (see page 59) the waist edges of the skirt fronts and skirt back. This helps to stop the curved edges from stretching out of shape.

3 If you're having a pocket, attach this next (see steps 2–6 of Lined/reversible version, page 26).

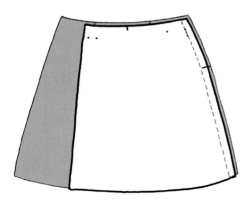

4 Place the right skirt front and skirt back right sides together. Making sure that the notches at the hipline match, pin the right side seam (the notched edge). Pin each end of the seam first, then match the notches, and finally pin the rest. (This seam crosses the bias in the fabric, meaning that one side can stretch easily if you start pinning at one end of the seam, resulting in mis-matched seams by the time you get to the other end.) Baste (tack) the seam, then machine stitch and press open (see Seams, page 136).

5 Repeat with the left side seam, but leave a gap in the stitching between the dots if you're having ties (you don't need to leave the gap for the button or D-ring versions). For the D-ring version, position the short tie between the dots on the back skirt and baste in place before then joining the left side seam as described in step 4, reverse stitching over the tie when machining the left side seam for added strength. Press the seam open.

Lined/reversible version with pocket

(works best with tie fastening): stitching darts, staystitching, attaching pocket, stitching side seams, making the ties, attaching the lining

1 Complete steps 1 and 2 of the instructions for all skirt versions, using the outer skirt only.

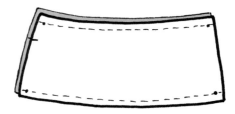

2 If you're having a pocket, place the two pocket bands right sides touching, pin together along the top and bottom long edges, baste, and machine.

3 Clip the curves (see Seams, page 138), press the seams open, and turn right side out.

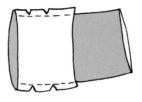

4 Press the pocket flat so that the top and bottom seams are flat and smooth. Position the pocket on the right/upper skirt front, with the top and bottom edges of the pocket level with the dots on the skirt front. Make sure you have the pocket the right way round—there should be a notch on one side of the pocket that matches up with the notch on the side seam edge of the skirt front.

5 Pin the pocket in position and baste it to the right/upper skirt front along the bottom of the pocket and the two short edges. Machine along the bottom edge of the pocket only, trying to keep a nice even distance in from the edge of the pocket; an edgestitch foot helps (see tips, below). The two short sides of the pocket are just basted for now, as they will be sewn into the seams later.

EDGESTITCHING

Edgestitching is topstitching (see Topstitching, page 138) along the finished edge of a garment. It helps flatten edges and give then a nice crisp, sharp shape, and is a detail often found on collars and cuffs. Used on the tie, it helps it to keep its shape and can add a bit of strength, too.

*

Ideally your machine stitching should be only approx. ⅛ in. (3 mm) in from the edge of the fabric. Using an edgestitch foot can help you to do this accurately.

*

If you don't have an edgestitch foot, you might find it easier to position the edgestitching a little further away from the edge (up to ¼ in./5 mm) and find something on your machine or presser foot to line up with the edge of the fabric to help you keep your stitching straight.

6 If you want to divide the long pocket band into separate pockets, mark your stitch lines with chalk and machine along them.

7 Continue to make up the outer skirt by following steps 4 and 5 for all versions.

8 Repeat steps 1–5 (as for all versions) with the lining (with or without the pocket), but leave the gap described in step 5 in the right side seam; this will actually become the left side seam when worn, because you effectively wear a lining inside out.

9 Make the short tie: with right sides together, fold the short tie piece in half lengthwise. Pin together along the long raw edges and one short edge, then machine (see Seams, page 136).

10 Press the seam allowances at the corners over each other.

11 Turn through to the right side—use the blunt end of a knitting needle to help push the seamed short end down inside the tie to start turning through.

12 Press and edgestitch all the edges except the short open end (see step 5 for more detailed instructions on edgestitching).

13 Repeat steps 9–12 with the long tie.

14 Instead of making ties, you can use cotton herringbone tape cut to the lengths of the pattern pieces and hem one short end.

TIP

If you would rather have a simple square patch pocket instead of a band, use the pocket band pattern to create the depth of your pocket and make it in the same way, basting along the bottom and 2 sides, and machining along the bottom edge and side that's not against the side seam. I think they're nice with the second side caught in the side seam.

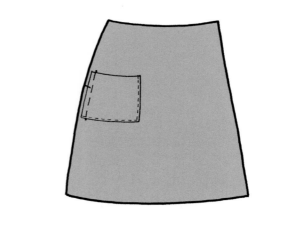

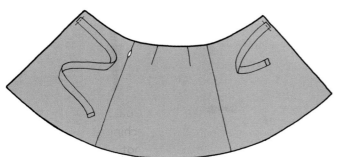

15 Baste the ties into position on the outer skirt. Place long tie on the right side of the fabric, on the left/under front skirt at the opening edge; position the top edge of the tie level with the dot, making sure you are attaching the open (un-seamed) end of the tie. The short tie goes in the same position at the opening edge of the right/upper front.

16 To join the outer and the lining: place the outer skirt and lining right sides together. Pin, baste, and machine the two layers together around the waist edge and the two front opening edges, leaving the hem open. At the front opening edges, reverse stitch over the ties for extra strength.

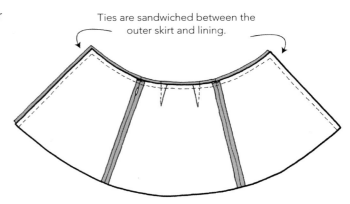

Ties are sandwiched between the outer skirt and lining.

17 Clip the curves on the waist seam (see Seams, page 138) and press the whole of the seam (the waist and the front opening edges) open as far as possible. At the corners of the waist and the front opening edges, fold the seam allowances toward the lining (over the top of each other at right angles), and press. This will give you a much sharper corner when you then turn the fabric through to the right side.

18 Turn the skirt right side out and press the seams flat. Line up the openings in the left side seams of the outer skirt and lining, and pin the outer and lining skirts together. Machine stitch a rectangle around the opening to hold it in place.

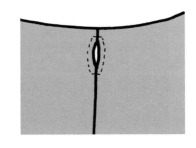

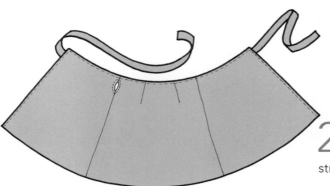

19 Hem the skirt next (see All Versions: Hemming, page 33), before doing the edgestitching, otherwise the edgestitching will prevent you from being able to stitch the hem properly at the front opening edges.

20 Edgestitch the waist and the two front opening edges to keep them flat, give them definition, and strengthen them (see step 5 for edgestitching instructions).

Button fastening version with facing: marking buttonhole positions, attaching facing, stitching side seams

1 Trim ¼ in. (5 mm) from the front and back waist facing pieces that you cut out in interfacing so that they are a bit smaller than the fabric pieces. Following the manufacturer's instructions, attach the interfacing pieces to the wrong side of the fabric front and back waist facings. Use a muslin pressing cloth to protect your iron and fabric.

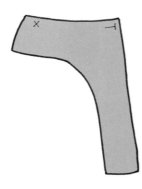

2 Mark the buttonhole and button positions on the front waist facing pieces: mark them with chalk on the wrong side of the facing, then with basting stitches in a contrasting color thread so that you can see them on the right side of the facing.

3 With right sides together, matching the notches, pin the front waist facings to the back waist facing at the side seams. Machine the seams (see Seams, page 136), press the seams open, and neaten all the way around the inner (un-notched) edge of the facings. If you prefer, you can finish this edge with bias binding (see Seams—Neatening Seam Allowances, Bias Binding, page 137).

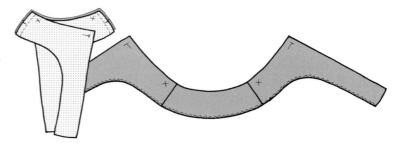

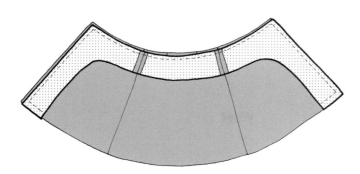

4 With right sides together, making sure the side seams and notches match, place the facing strip on the skirt and pin together along the waist, down the two front opening edges and across the hem of the facing strip. Baste and machine stitch (see Seams, page 136). Remember when joining the bottom (hem) of the facing and skirt that the hem allowance is ¾ in./2 cm (see Attaching Waist Facings, page 146).

5 Press the seam toward the facing (don't worry about the corners, we'll come back to them in the next step), clip the curve of the waist seam, and understitch (see Seams, page 138) as far as possible; you won't be able to get right into the corners.

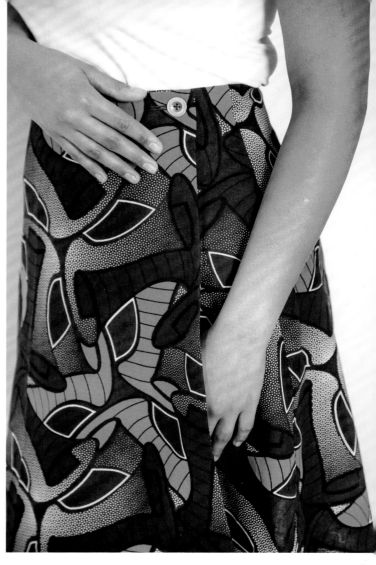

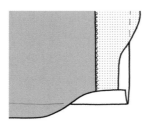

6 At the bottom corner of the front opening edge and the hem, fold the seam allowance and the hem allowance toward the facing (over the top of each other at right angles) and press them. This will give you a much sharper corner when you then turn the fabric through to the right side.

7 Repeat step 6 with the corners of the front opening edge and the waist.

8 Press the waist and front opening edges flat from the right side.

9 Work a buttonhole at both front opening edges at the waist in the position marked on your facing (see Buttons and Buttonholes, page 150).

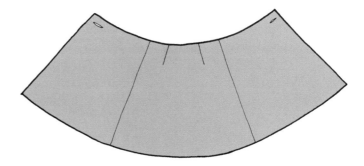

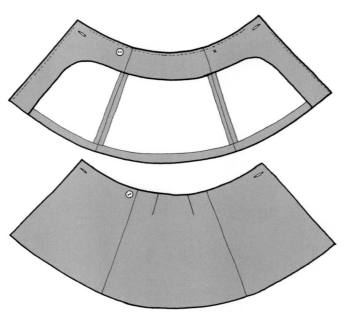

10 Attach buttons on the outside of the skirt on the left/under front and the inside of the skirt on the right/upper front in the marked positions (see Buttons and Buttonholes, page 150).

11 If you don't want to use buttons, replace steps 9 and 10 by attaching sew-on popper snaps in the marked positions.

D-ring fastening version with facing: attaching ties and D-rings

1 To make the short tie (to go in the left side seam), follow steps 9–12 of the lined/reversible version.

2 Make your D-ring tab in the same way, but only join the long side and keep both short ends open.

3 Instead of making your tie and D-ring tab, you can use cotton herringbone tape cut to the lengths of the pattern pieces.

4 Insert the short tie into the left side seam, following step 5 of All Versions.

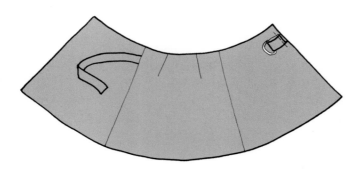

5 Feed the D-rings onto the D-ring tab and fold the tab in half. Place the raw edges of the folded tab level with the front opening edge of the right/upper front skirt, so that the top edge of the tab is level with the dot, and baste in place.

6 Then follow steps 1 and 3–8 of the button fastening version, sandwiching the D-ring tab in the front opening edge of the right/upper front between the skirt and the facing. Reverse stitch over the tab when machining the right/upper front opening seam for added strength.

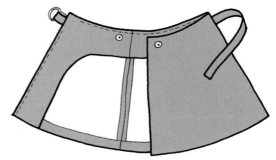

7 Finally, attach a sew-on popper snap to fix the opening edge of the left/under front to the underside of the right/upper front.

All versions: hemming

1 The hem of this skirt is slightly curved.
The Bias-faced Hem method (page 140)
gives this skirt a really neat finish.

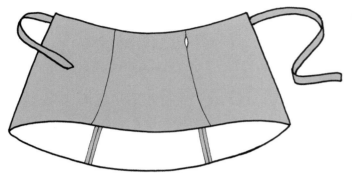

2 To hem the lined/reversible skirt: the two hems
hang loose from each other, but are attached at
the front opening edges, which forms one big circle.
Hem all the way around this big circle.

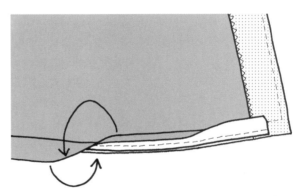

3 To hem the faced skirt: turn the bottom of the
facing back to reveal the wrong side of the facing
at the hem. Attach the beginning of the bias binding
to the right side of the skirt hem, extending by approx.
¾ in. (2 cm) onto the facing at each end of the hem.
Turn the facing back through to the right side and
allow the hem of the skirt to start to turn up.

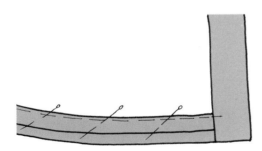

4 Make sure the hem of the skirt is turning up
by ¾ in. (2 cm) and pin the hem and bias
binding in place. Baste close to the top loose edge
of the bias binding.

5 Press the hem in place to remove any
excess fabric and machine, then remove
the basting stitches.

CHANGING THE SIZE
OF THE TIES

You can make the ties wider, but don't go
narrower (they're currently 1 in./2.5 cm wide when
finished). If you do widen them, remember to
increase the size of the opening for the tie in the
left side seam.

HOLLINGS—THE CIRCLE SKIRT

As soon as I put on a circle skirt, I want to twirl about like a little girl! What's better, they are one of the easiest skirt patterns to draft, which is why I haven't included a pattern. Instead, I'm going to show you how to draft one to your own measurements.

Make a circle skirt for everyday wear using a solid fabric and going for knee length. A shorter-length version in a printed cotton with an elasticated waist will be easy to wear on a summer vacation. And what could be more dramatic than a floor-length circle skirt for special occasions? So decadent and my personal favorite way to wear a circle skirt—although I decided to give mine a twist with a raised front hem.

Last but not least, it's the perfect skirt for a side seam pocket—the easiest type of pocket to have a go at if you have never attempted pockets before.

As you are going to be drafting this pattern yourself, there are no pattern pieces to trace and no size charts. All you need is your waist measurement and a length for your finished skirt.

DRAFTING YOUR PATTERN

You will need

- Large piece of paper (specialist pattern paper, newspaper, wallpaper lining paper, and greaseproof paper are all suitable)—you may need to stick several pieces of paper together if a single sheet is not large enough
- Pencil
- Long ruler (meter)
- Calculator (don't worry, only to work out one number!)
- Paper scissors
- Tape measure
- Set square

Make a note of these measurements: your waist and the length you want the finished skirt to be (see Sizing & Taking Measurements, page 130).

WITH THIS SKIRT, YOU WILL PRACTICE THE FOLLOWING BASIC TECHNIQUES:

- Seams
- Hems
- Using elastic
- Attaching waistbands
- Inserting zippers
- Adding pockets

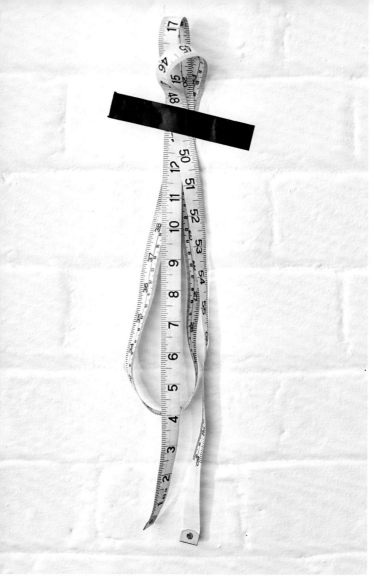

Basic version

1 We're going to draft a quarter of a circle. On a large piece of paper, draw two lines at right angles to each other.

2 To draw in the waistline of the skirt, you need to work out the radius of your waist measurement. (Don't worry! This is the only serious math bit.) To do that, divide your waist measurement by 6.28. Here's an example using my waist measurement: 31½ in. (80 cm) divided by 6.28 = 5 in. (12.7 cm).

3 From the intersection of your two initial straight lines, mark the distance worked out in step 2 on both straight lines.

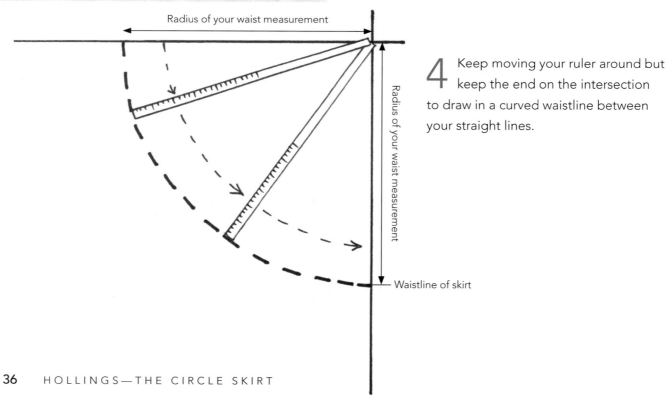

Radius of your waist measurement

Radius of your waist measurement

Waistline of skirt

4 Keep moving your ruler around but keep the end on the intersection to draw in a curved waistline between your straight lines.

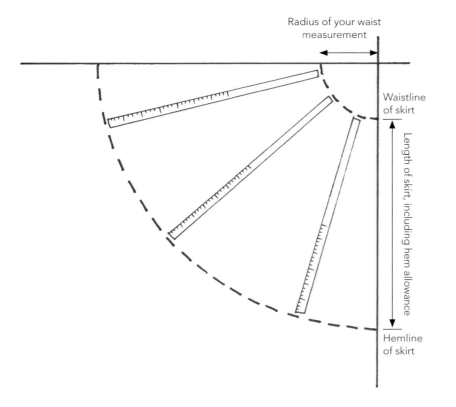

Radius of your waist measurement

Waistline of skirt

Length of skirt, including hem allowance

Hemline of skirt

5 Next, you need to draw the hemline of your skirt. Work out what length you want the skirt to be once finished and add a ⅜-in. (1-cm) hem allowance. Starting from the waistline, mark the skirt length, moving your ruler around the waistline curve to draw in a smooth, curved hemline.

> **TIP**
>
> Good lengths are on the knee, just below the knee, ankle length, or mid thigh.

6 That's the basic skirt done! Now you just need to add the seam allowances. Add ⅝ in. (1.5 cm) above the waistline and outside each of the straight lines. (The seam allowances are drawn as a broken line here.) Also add the grain line arrow (see Using Paper Patterns, page 131) parallel to the center front and center back line. Add a double notch onto the side seams exactly the same distance above the hemline on the front and back skirt pattern pieces (two small lines on the side-seam cutting line). These will help you identify which are the side seams and which are the center front and center back seams later when you're putting your skirt together. You can either trace the skirt onto a new piece of paper to do this or add them to the pattern you have just drafted. This pattern piece is a quarter of your skirt, so you will need to cut it out four times in your chosen fabric (two front skirt pieces and two back skirt pieces).

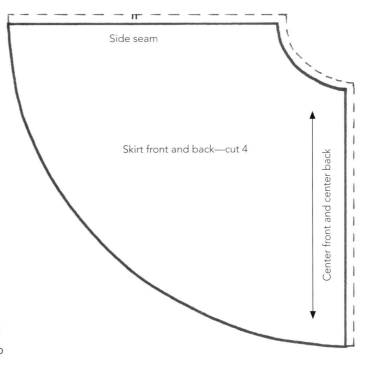

Side seam

Skirt front and back—cut 4

Center front and center back

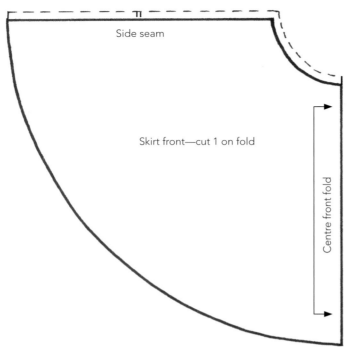

Side seam

Skirt front—cut 1 on fold

Centre front fold

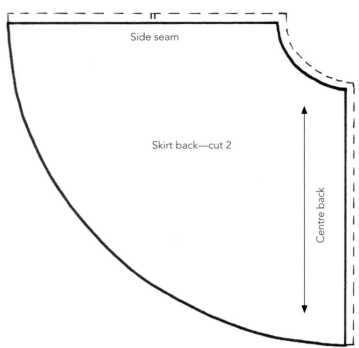

Side seam

Skirt back—cut 2

Centre back

7 If your fabric is wide enough for you to cut your pattern piece with the fabric folded, you only need to add a seam allowance to the side seam and center back (we will work out how your pattern will fit on your fabric later, so be aware that you might need to come back to this). You will need two pattern pieces—one back that will be cut twice and have a seam allowance along both straight edges, and one front that will be cut once on the fold of the fabric and will only have a seam allowance along the side seam line, not the center front line. Note that the grain line arrow is drawn differently on the front skirt when the center front is placed on a fold; the ends are turned in to point at the center front line. Make sure you read Using Paper Patterns (page 131), which explains grain lines in more detail.

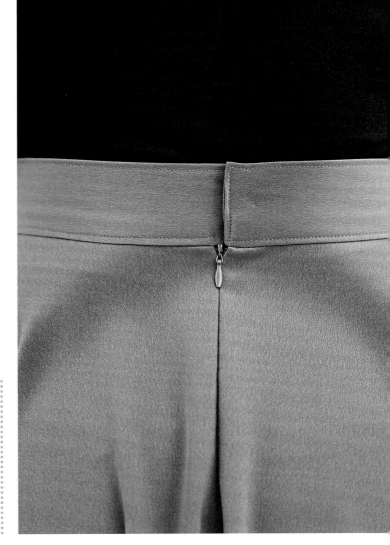

1½-in. (4-cm)
underwrap for
fastening

Waist measurement used to draft your skirt

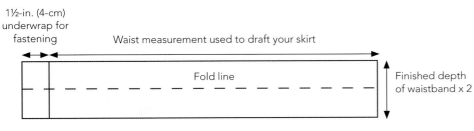

Fold line

Finished depth
of waistband x 2

8 All you need to do now is draft a waistband. Draw a rectangle: the length should be the waist measurement you used to draft your skirt, and the width should be twice the depth you want the finished waistband to be. Add 1½ in. (4 cm) onto one end for the waistband to fasten.

9 Add a ⅝-in. (1.5-cm) seam allowance all the way around. You'll cut one waistband in fabric and one in interfacing.

Add a ⅝-in. (1.5-cm) seam allowance all the way around

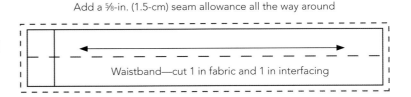

Waistband—cut 1 in fabric and 1 in interfacing

Elasticated waist version

To draft the elasticated waist version, follow steps 1–7 of the basic version, but base all the measurements on your hip measurement rather than your waist measurement so that you can pull the skirt on over your hips without the need for a zipper! Don't draft a waistband.

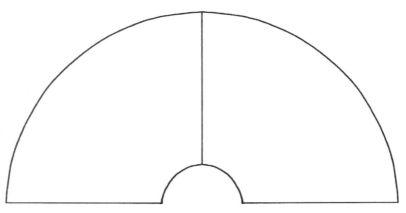

Raised front hem version

1 To draft the raised front hem version, follow steps 1–5 of the basic version to your required front skirt length and stop before you add the seam allowances. Trace a copy of the skirt pattern, cut out the tracing and the original, and place them on a new piece of paper, touching along one long edge to form a half circle.

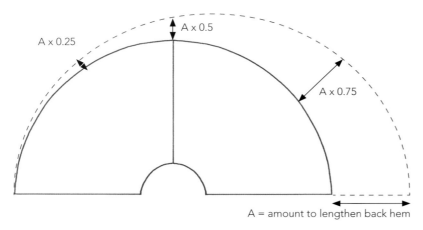

A x 0.5

A x 0.25

A x 0.75

A = amount to lengthen back hem

2 To create the curved hem, work out how much you need to add to make the back skirt the length you want. Add half of this amount at the side seams, a quarter of the amount halfway between the center front and the side seam, and three-quarters of the amount halfway between the center back and the side seam. Draw a neat, curved line linking up all these points.

3 Trace the front and back separately and add a ⅝-in. (1.5-cm) seam allowance to the waistline, side seam, center front, and center back.

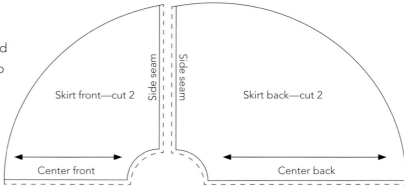

Skirt front—cut 2

Side seam

Side seam

Skirt back—cut 2

Center front

Center back

To draft a pocket

NOTE: these pockets only work with a fixed waistband, not with an elasticated waist.

1 On your skirt pattern piece, draw a pocket shape and an opening big enough to fit your hand. The top of the pocket opening should be approx. 4 in. (10 cm) below the waistline and the length of the opening approx. 5 in. (12 cm). Make sure that the pocket bag is generously sized and big enough to fit your hand. Copy the dots for the pocket opening position onto the skirt pattern piece.

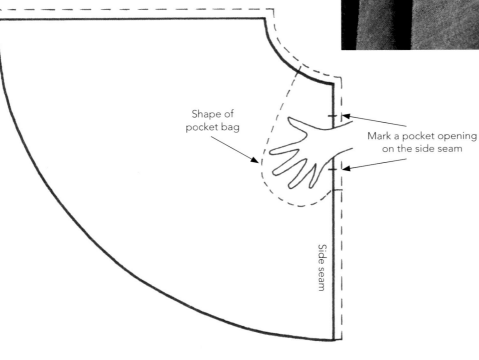

Shape of pocket bag

Mark a pocket opening on the side seam

Side seam

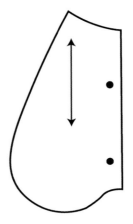

2 Trace the pocket pattern piece. You will need to cut this four times (so that you have two pairs—a left and right pocket piece for both the front and the back of the skirt) in fabric.

WHAT FABRIC SHOULD I USE?

A circle skirt works best in densely woven fabrics so that the hem can't drop out of shape. Crisp cotton poplins and chambray, lightweight denim, satin, and crêpe are all ideal.

The skirt works well in solid colors or abstract prints, but it isn't ideal for one-way prints, fabrics with a surface texture or pile such as corduroy, or stripes, as the positioning of the pattern pieces on the fabric can result in one-way prints looking lopsided and stripes being distorted.

My samples are made in the following fabrics:

• Plain denim knee-length version with pockets: cotton lightweight denim

• Splatter print short elasticated waist version: cotton poplin

• Raised front hem gray version: polyester crêpe

If you are unsure whether a fabric is suitable, check the Fabrics Glossary (page 157).

WORKING OUT FABRIC AMOUNTS

Cutting the front skirt on a fold, without a center seam

If the front skirt can be cut on a fold, it will not need a center seam. To find out if this is possible, you need to work out the longest length that you can make your skirt with the fabric folded lengthwise.

The formula for working this out is:
Maximum skirt length = half the width of the fabric minus the radius of your waist (see step 2 of Drafting Your Pattern—Basic Version)

Here's an example:
Half the width of my fabric = 29½ in. (75 cm)
Radius used to draft my skirt = 5 in. (12.7 cm)
29½ in. (75 cm) minus 5 in. (12.7 cm) = 24½ in. (62.3 cm)
So cutting my fabric folded lengthwise, the maximum skirt length that I can have, including the hem allowance, is 24½ in. (62.3 cm).

Cutting the front skirt as two pieces, with a center seam

If your fabric is too narrow to fit on your required skirt length with the fabric folded in half lengthwise, you can fold it widthwise. This means that the skirt front will need to have a center front seam.

The formula for working this out is:
Maximum skirt length = full width of the fabric minus the radius of the waist (see step 2 of Drafting Your Pattern—Basic Version)

Here's an example:
Full width of my fabric = 45 in. (115 cm)
Radius used to draft my skirt = 5 in. (12.7 cm)
45 in. (115 cm) minus 5 in. (12.7 cm) = 40 in. (102.3 cm)
So cutting my fabric folded widthwise, the maximum skirt length that I can have, including the hem allowance, is 40 in. (102.3 cm).

As you can see, longer skirts usually need to be cut with the fabric folded widthwise, requiring much more fabric. I had to do this with my gray raised front hem version, which used 4⅜ yd (4 m) of fabric!

CHOOSING A CUTTING PLAN

Once you've worked out how your pattern will fit on your fabric, you can choose a cutting plan:

• Wide fabric folded lengthwise—follow cutting plan 1 or 2, whichever your pattern will fit.

• Narrow fabric folded widthwise—follow cutting plan 3.

• Narrow fabric unfolded—follow cutting plan 4.

YOU WILL NEED
In addition to fabric, you will need:

Versions with a waistband

• 8-in. (20-cm) regular closed-end zipper or 9-in. (23-cm) invisible zipper (using a slightly longer invisible zipper will make it easier to insert)

• 8 in. (20 cm) light- or medium-weight iron-on interfacing (lightweight for satin, crêpe, medium-weight for poplin, denim)

• 1 x hook and bar or button (min. ⅝ in./1.5 cm diameter)

Elasticated waist version

• Elastic 1¼ in. (3 cm) wide—enough to comfortably fit your waist

All versions

• Matching sewing thread

PREPARING YOUR PATTERN PIECES
Draft the pattern pieces in the size you need—skirt front and skirt back (in short or full length), and waistband and pocket bags (if required). Read the instructions in Using Paper Patterns, page 131.

CUTTING YOUR FABRIC
Make sure you read the Fabrics section (page 132) before you lay out your pattern pieces and take the scissors to your fabric!

Following the cutting plan for your fabric width, pin the pattern pieces to the fabric. Cut out all pieces

in fabric, then cut out the waistband (if using) again in interfacing. Your interfacing may not be wide enough to fit the full length of the waistband pattern piece, if so, cut the waistband in 2 parts. Transfer any markings to the fabric (see page 133).

Cutting plan 1

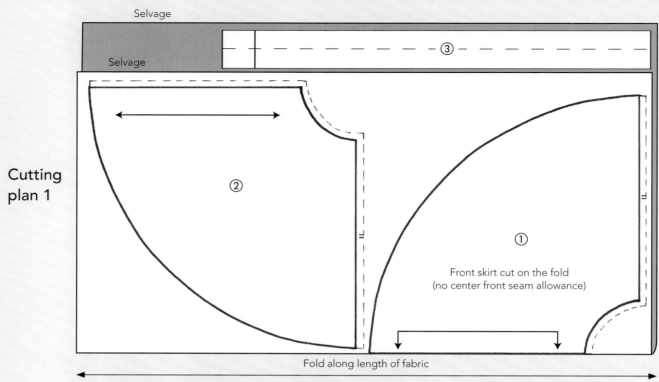

Selvage

Selvage

②

① Front skirt cut on the fold
(no center front seam allowance)

③

Fold along length of fabric

Measure the length once you've laid out your pattern pieces to work out how much fabric you will need to make your skirt

Pattern pieces

① Skirt front

② Skirt back

③ Waistband

Key

Fabric

Right side   Wrong side

Pattern pieces

Printed side up   Printed side down

Cutting plan 2

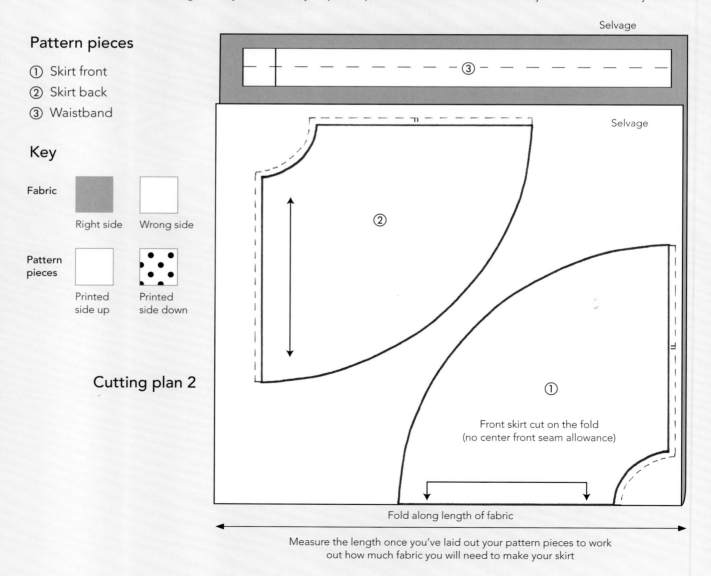

Selvage

Selvage

②

③

① Front skirt cut on the fold
(no center front seam allowance)

Fold along length of fabric

Measure the length once you've laid out your pattern pieces to work out how much fabric you will need to make your skirt

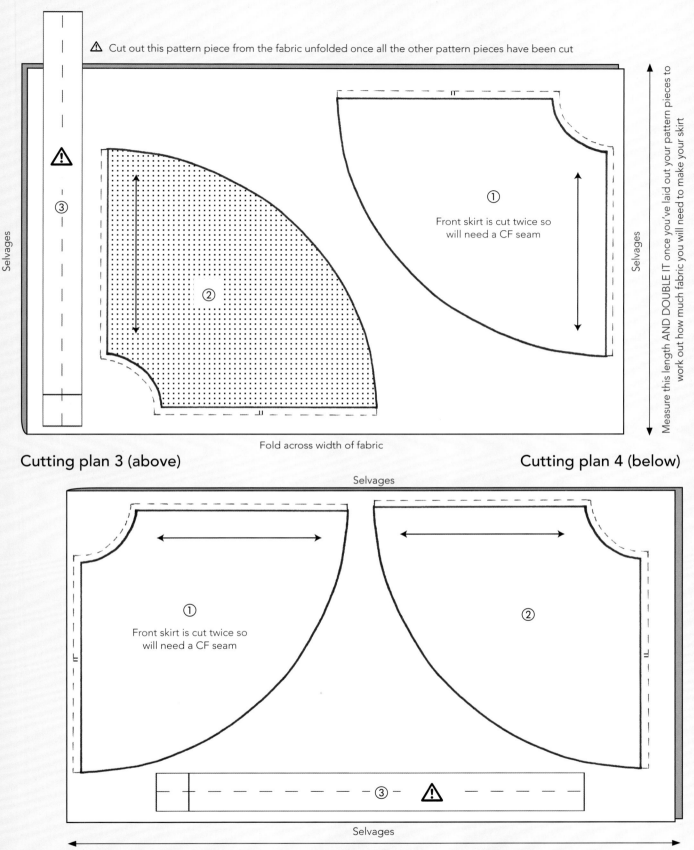

⚠ Cut out this pattern piece from the fabric unfolded once all the other pattern pieces have been cut

① Front skirt is cut twice so will need a CF seam

② ③

Selvages

Measure this length AND DOUBLE IT once you've laid out your pattern pieces to work out how much fabric you will need to make your skirt

Fold across width of fabric

Cutting plan 3 (above)

Cutting plan 4 (below)

Selvages

① Front skirt is cut twice so will need a CF seam

②

③ ⚠

Selvages

Measure the length AND DOUBLE IT once you've laid out your pattern pieces to work out how much fabric you will need to make your skirt

⚠ Cut out this pattern piece from the fabric unfolded once all the other pattern pieces have been cut

PUTTING IT TOGETHER

Seam allowance is ⅝ in. (1.5 cm)
Hem allowance is ⅜ in. (1 cm)

Key to diagrams
Shaded = right side of fabric
White = wrong side of fabric

Basic version with waistband (any length)

1 Trim ¼ in. (5 mm) from the waistband piece that you cut out in interfacing so that it is a bit smaller than the fabric piece. Following the manufacturer's instructions, attach the interfacing piece to the wrong side of the fabric waistband. Use a muslin pressing cloth to protect your iron and fabric.

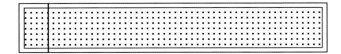

2 If you have a center front seam, join this first. With the right sides of the fabric together, pin the front pieces together along the center front seam (the center front is the straight edge without any notches). Baste (tack), machine the seam, and neaten the raw edges (see Seams, page 136).

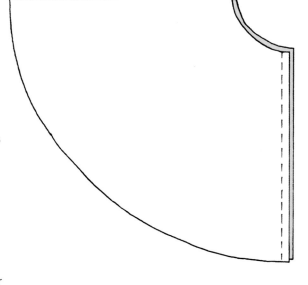

3 If you are having in-seam pockets, attach the pocket bags first to all four side-seam edges. Place the pockets with the right side of the fabric against the right side of the skirt piece and match up the pocket-opening dots, making sure that the straight edge of the pocket and the straight edge of the skirt are level (see Pockets—In-Seam, page 153).

4 Insert either a centered or an invisible zipper in the center back of the skirt (see Zippers, page 143). If this is your first zipper, choose a centered, not an invisible, zipper.

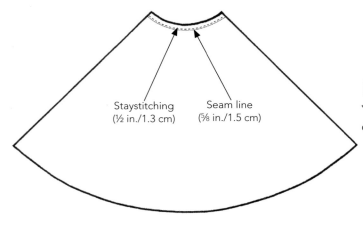

Staystitching
(½ in./1.3 cm)

Seam line
(⅝ in./1.5 cm)

5 Staystitch the waist edges of the skirt front and back pieces (see page 59). This helps to stop the curved edges from stretching out of shape.

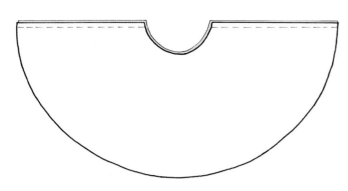

6 Place the skirt front and skirt back right sides together and pin the side seams, make sure that the notches match. Pin each end of each seam first, then match the notches, and finally pin the rest. (This seam crosses the bias in the fabric, meaning that one side can stretch easily if you start pinning at one end of the seam, resulting in mis-matched seams by the time you get to the other end.) Baste the side seams securely and machine stitch (see Seams, page 136). If you are having pockets in your version, refer to Pockets—In-Seam, page 153 for details of how to sew around the pocket bags when you join the side seams.

7 Attach the waistband to the skirt (see Attaching Waistbands, page 147).

Elasticated waist version

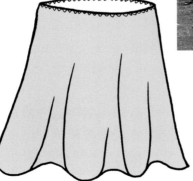

1 Follow steps 2 and 6 for the basic version.

2 Neaten the waist edge of the skirt with a zigzag stitch (see Seams—Neatening Seam Allowances, page 137).

3 Attach the elastic to the waist edge (see Using Elastic—Exposed Elastic Waistband, page 141).

All versions: hemming

Curved hems are notoriously difficult to do. I find the best way to do them is using the Bias-faced Hem method (see Hems, page 140).

RUSHOLME—THE A-LINE SKIRT

I don't know many people who don't suit an A-line skirt. It's such a great shape and deserves a place as a staple go-to skirt in your closet.

Flattering and comfortable, A-line skirts work well in a wide range of fabrics and, depending on the details and fabric you use, you can create lots of different looks. In lightweight wools with a lining, an A-line can be a smart skirt for the office, while a shorter version in denim looks great with contrast topstitching and is perfect with either bare legs and sneakers in summer or warm, wooly tights and boots in winter. My longer-length camel-colored corduroy version with pockets is a great '70s throwback that still looks on trend today.

There are lots of different ways to make this skirt: completely plain, with a faced waist or a waistband, with a center front pleat, or with cut-away front hip pockets (which are actually a lot easier to sew than many people think).

Start with a plain version and move on to adding the pleat and pockets as you gain confidence.

Follow the instructions in Sizing & Taking Measurements (page 130) for exactly where and how to measure yourself and how to choose which size to make.

FINISHED SKIRT MEASUREMENTS

Size (Your actual hip measurement)

	34¾ in. (88 cm)	36¼ in. (92 cm)	38 in. (96 cm)	39½ in. (100 cm)	41 in. (104 cm)	43 in. (109 cm)	45 in. (114 cm)	47 in. (119 cm)	49 in. (124 cm)	51 in. (129 cm)
Waist	25½ in. (65 cm)	27 in. (69 cm)	28¾ in. (73 cm)	30½ in. (77 cm)	32 in. (81 cm)	34 in. (86 cm)	36 in. (91 cm)	38 in. (96 cm)	40 in. (101 cm)	42 in. (106 cm)
Hips	38 in. (97 cm)	40 in. (101 cm)	41½ in. (105 cm)	43 in. (109 cm)	44½ in. (113 cm)	46½ in. (118 cm)	48½ in. (123 cm)	50½ in. (128 cm)	52½ in. (133 cm)	54 ½ in. (138 cm)
Length from waist seam down center back (short version)	21 in. (53.5 cm)	21½ in. (54.5 cm)	22 in. (55.5 cm)	22¼ in. (56.5 cm)	22¾ in. (57.5 cm)	23 in. (58.5 cm)	23½ in. (59.5 cm)	24 in. (60.5 cm)	24¼ in. (61.5 cm)	24¾ in. (62.5 cm)
Length from waist seam down center back (knee-length version)	22¾ in. (57.5 cm)	23 in. (58.5 cm)	23½ in. (59.5 cm)	24 in. (60.5 cm)	24¼ in. (61.5 cm)	24¾ in. (62.5 cm)	25 in. (63.5 cm)	25½ in. (64.5 cm)	25¾ in. (65.5 cm)	26¼ in. (66.5 cm)
Length from waist seam down center (long version)	24½ in. (61.5 cm)	24¾ in. (62.5 in.)	25 in. (63.5 cm)	25½ in. (64.5 cm)	25¾ in. (65.5 cm)	26¼ in. (66.5 cm)	26½ in. (67.5 cm)	27 in. (68.5 cm)	27½ in. (69.5 cm)	27¾ in. (70.5 cm)

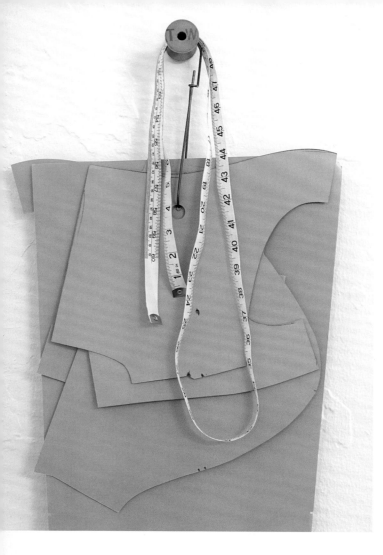

My samples are made in the following fabrics:

• Short denim version with topstitching: cotton denim

• Knee-length feather print version with center front pleat: cotton/elastane stretch cotton sateen

• Long corduroy version with pockets: cotton needlecord (remember that corduroy has a nap, or pile, which can affect the amount of fabric you need and how the pattern pieces are cut. See Fabrics, page 132—and if this is your first skirt, maybe avoid corduroy to start with!)

If you are unsure whether a fabric is suitable, check the Fabrics Glossary (page 157).

This pattern is suitable for one-way prints and fabrics with a surface texture or pile.

YOU WILL NEED

For all versions

Matching sewing thread
8½-in. (22-cm) regular closed-end zipper or 9-in. (23-cm) invisible zipper (using a slightly longer invisible zipper will make it easier to insert)

For waistband version

1 x hook and bar or button (min. ⅝ in./1.5 cm diameter)

WHAT FABRIC SHOULD I USE?

An A-line skirt looks great in medium-weight woven fabrics such as denims, linen, cotton/linen blends, corduroy, velvet, cotton chintz, cotton poplin, lightweight wools, and stretch woven fabrics that have some elastane. It will work well in either solid colors or prints.

It isn't really suited to very lightweight fabrics such as satin and crêpe. Do not choose a knitted fabric.

Rusholme short version with waist facing and optional center front seam

NOTE: To add **pockets** or a **pleat**, or to make with a **waistband** rather than a waist facing, add 10 in. (25 cm) to the fabric requirements.

FABRIC REQUIREMENTS

	Size (Your actual hip measurement)									
Fabric width	34¾ in. (88 cm)	36¼ in. (92 cm)	38 in. (96 cm)	39½ in. (100 cm)	41 in. (104 cm)	43 in. (109 cm)	45 in. (114 cm)	47 in. (119 cm)	49 in. (124 cm)	51 in. (129 cm)
44 in. (112 cm) or wider	1¾ yd (1.6 m)	1¾ yd (1.6 m)	1¾ yd (1.6 m)	1¾ yd (1.6 m)	1¾ yd (1.6 m)	1¾ yd (1.6 m)	1¾ yd (1.6 m)	1¾ yd (1.6 m)	1¾ yd (1.6 m)	1¾ yd (1.6 m)
55 in. (140 cm) or wider	1⅛ yd (1 m) *	1⅛ yd (1 m) *	1⅛ yd (1 m) *	1⅛ yd (1 m) *	1⅛ yd (1 m) *	1⅛ yd (1 m) *	1⅛ yd (1 m) *	1½ yd (1.3 m)	1½ yd (1.3 m)	1½ yd (1.3 m)
Interfacing (36 in./90 cm wide)	10 in. (25 cm)	10 in. (25 cm)	10 in. (25 cm)	10 in. (25 cm)	10 in. (25 cm)	16 in. (40 cm)	16 in. (40 cm)	16 in. (40 cm)	16 in. (40 cm)	16 in. (40 cm)

* Not suitable for directional prints or fabrics with a pile or surface texture (nap); if using one of these fabrics, you will need 1½ yd (1.3 m).

WHICH CUTTING PLAN TO FOLLOW

	Size (Your actual hip measurement)									
Fabric width	34¾ in. (88 cm)	36¼ in. (92 cm)	38 in. (96 cm)	39½ in. (100 cm)	41 in. (104 cm)	43 in. (109 cm)	45 in. (114 cm)	47 in. (119 cm)	49 in. (124 cm)	51 in. (129 cm)
44 in. (112 cm) or wider	1	1	1	1	1	1	1	1	1	1
55 in. (140 cm) or wider	2*	2*	2*	2*	2*	2*	2*	3	3	3
Interfacing (36 in./90 cm wide)	9	9	9	9	9	10	10	10	10	10

* Only follow cutting plan 2 if you are NOT using a directional print or a fabric with a pile (nap); if you are using one of these fabrics, follow cutting plan 3.

Rusholme knee-length version with waistband and center front pleat

NOTE: To add **pockets**, add 10 in. (25 cm) to the fabric requirements.

FABRIC REQUIREMENTS

Size (Your actual hip measurement)

Fabric width	34¾ in. (88 cm)	36¼ in. (92 cm)	38 in. (96 cm)	39½ in. (100 cm)	41 in. (104 cm)	43 in. (109 cm)	45 in. (114 cm)	47 in. (119 cm)	49 in. (124 cm)	51 in. (129 cm)
44 in. (112 cm) or wider	1⅞ yd (1.7 m)	1⅞ yd (1.7 m)	1⅞ yd (1.7 m)	1⅞ yd (1.7 m)	1⅞ yd (1.7 m)	1⅞ yd (1.7 m)	1⅞ yd (1.7 m)	1¾ yd (1.5 m) *	1¾ yd (1.5 m) *	1¾ yd (1.5 m) *
55 in. (140 cm) or wider	1⅝ yd (1.4 m)	1⅝ yd (1.4 m)	1⅝ yd (1.4 m)	1⅝ yd (1.4 m)	1⅝ yd (1.4 m)	1⅝ yd (1.4 m)	1⅝ yd (1.4 m)	1⅝ yd (1.4 m)	1⅝ yd (1.4 m)	1⅝ yd (1.4 m)
Interfacing (36 in./90 cm wide)	10 in. (25 cm)	10 in. (25 cm)	10 in. (25 cm)	10 in. (25 cm)	10 in. (25 cm)	16 in. (40 cm)	16 in. (40 cm)	16 in. (40 cm)	16 in. (40 cm)	16 in. (40 cm)

* Not suitable for directional prints or fabrics with a pile (nap).

WHICH CUTTING PLAN TO FOLLOW

Size (Your actual hip measurement)

Fabric width	34¾ in. (88 cm)	36¼ in. (92 cm)	38 in. (96 cm)	39½ in. (100 cm)	41 in. (104 cm)	43 in. (109 cm)	45 in. (114 cm)	47 in. (119 cm)	49 in. (124 cm)	51 in. (129 cm)
44 in. (112 cm) or wider	4	4	4	4	4	4	4	5 *	5 *	5 *
55 in. (140 cm) or wider	6	6	6	6	6	6	6	6	6	6
Interfacing (36 in./90 cm wide)	11	11	11	11	11	12	12	12	12	¡12

* Not suitable for directional prints or fabrics with a pile or surface texture (nap).

Rusholme long version with pockets and waistband

NOTE: To add a **pleat**, add 10 in. (25 cm) to the fabric requirements.

FABRIC REQUIREMENTS

Size (Your actual hip measurement)

Fabric width	34¾ in. (88 cm)	36¼ in. (92 cm)	38 in. (96 cm)	39½ in. (100 cm)	41 in. (104 cm)	43 in. (109 cm)	45 in. (114 cm)	47 in. (119 cm)	49 in. (124 cm)	51 in. (129 cm)
44 in. (112 cm) or wider	2⅝ yd (2.4 m)	2⅝ yd (2.4 m)	2⅝ yd (2.4 m)	2⅝ yd (2.4 m)	2⅝ yd (2.4 m)	2⅝ yd (2.4 m)	2⅝ yd (2.4 m)	2⅝ yd (2.4 m)	2⅝ yd (2.4 m)	2⅝ yd (2.4 m)
55 in. (140 cm) or wider	2½ yd (2.2 m) *	2½ yd (2.2 m) *	2½ yd (2.2 m) *	2½ yd (2.2 m) *	2½ yd (2.2 m) *	2½ yd (2.2 m) *	2½ yd (2.2 m) *	2½ yd (2.2 m) *	2½ yd (2.2 m) *	2½ yd (2.2 m) *
Interfacing (36 in./90 cm wide)	10 in. (25 cm)	10 in. (25 cm)	10 in. (25 cm)	10 in. (25 cm)	10 in. (25 cm)	10 in. (25 cm)	10 in. (25 cm)	10 in. (25 cm)	10 in. (25 cm)	10 in. (25 cm)

* Not suitable for directional prints or fabrics with a pile (nap); if you are using one of these fabrics, you will need 2⅝ yd (2.4 m).

WHICH CUTTING PLAN TO FOLLOW

Size (Your actual hip measurement)

Fabric width	34¾ in. (88 cm)	36¼ in. (92 cm)	38 in. (96 cm)	39½ in. (100 cm)	41 in. (104 cm)	43 in. (109 cm)	45 in. (114 cm)	47 in. (119 cm)	49 in. (124 cm)	51 in. (129 cm)
44 in. (112 cm) or wider	7	7	7	7	7	7	7	7	7	7
55 in. (140 cm) or wider	8*	8*	8*	8*	8*	8*	8*	8*	8*	8*
Interfacing (36 in./90 cm wide)	11	11	11	11	11	12	12	12	12	12

* Only follow plan 8 if you are NOT using a directional print or fabric with a pile or surface texture (nap); if you are using one of these fabrics, follow cutting plan 7.

PREPARING YOUR PATTERN PIECES

Trace off the pattern pieces in the size you need from the pattern sheet—skirt front and skirt back, front and back waist facings (use front and back waist facing patterns from Fallowfield Pencil Skirt) or waistband (use waistband pattern from Fallowfield Pencil Skirt), and front facing/under pocket band and top pocket bag (if required). Read the instructions in Using Paper Patterns, page 131.

CUTTING YOUR FABRIC

Make sure you read the Fabrics section (page 132) before you lay out your pattern pieces and take the scissors to your fabric!

Following the cutting plan for your fabric width, pin the pattern pieces to the fabric. Cut out all pieces in fabric, then cut out the waist facings or waistband again in interfacing. Your interfacing may not be wide enough to fit the full length of the waistband pattern piece, if so cut the waistband in 2 parts (see Cutting Plan 12). Transfer any markings to the fabric (see page 133).

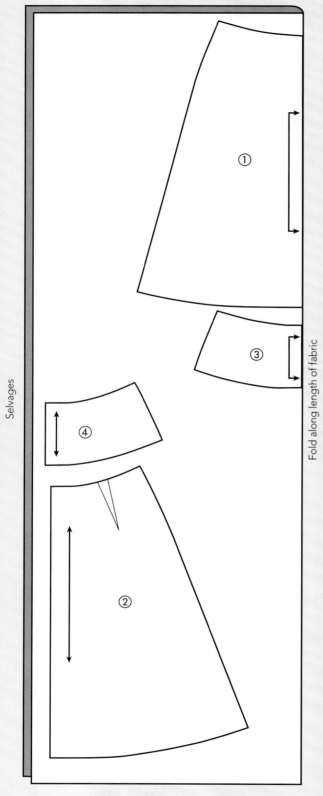

Pattern pieces

① Skirt front
② Skirt back
③ Front waist facing
④ Back waist facing
⑤ Waistband

Key

Fabric

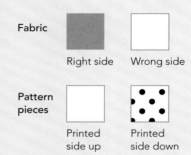

Right side   Wrong side

Pattern pieces

Printed side up   Printed side down

Cutting plan 1 (above)

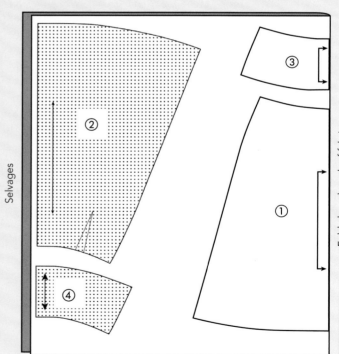

Cutting plan 2 (above)

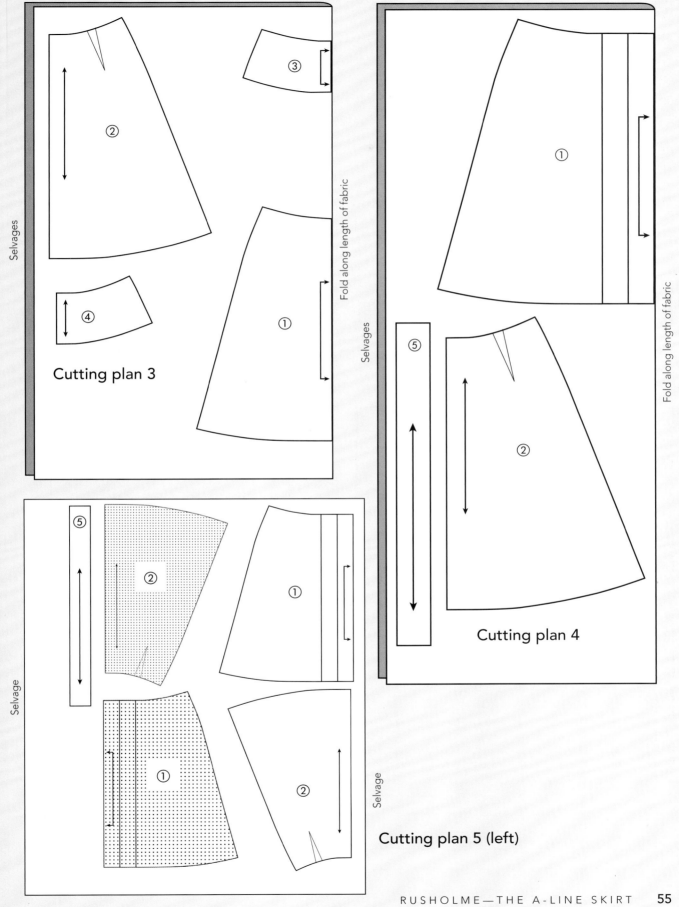

Cutting plan 3

Cutting plan 4

Cutting plan 5 (left)

Selvages

Fold along length of fabric

Selvages

Fold along length of fabric

Selvage

Selvage

Pattern pieces

① Skirt front
② Skirt back
③ Front waist facing
④ Back waist facing
⑤ Waistband
⑥ Front facing / underpocket
⑦ Top Pocket

Key

Fabric

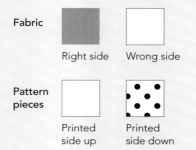

Right side   Wrong side

Pattern pieces

Printed side up   Printed side down

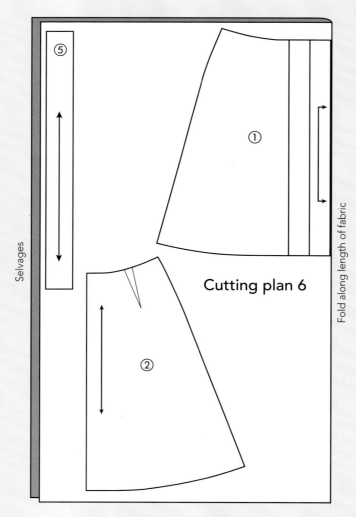

Cutting plan 6

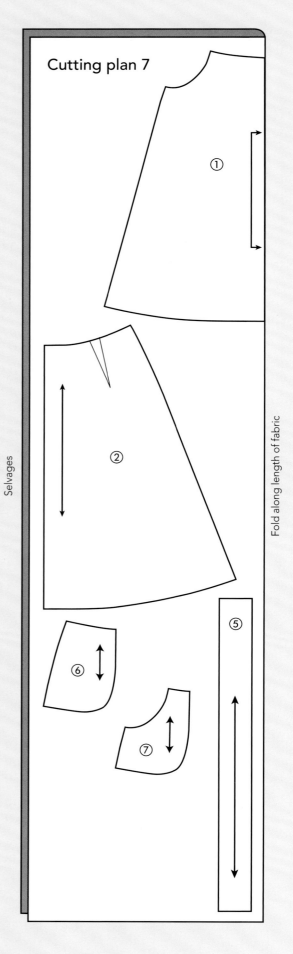

Cutting plan 7

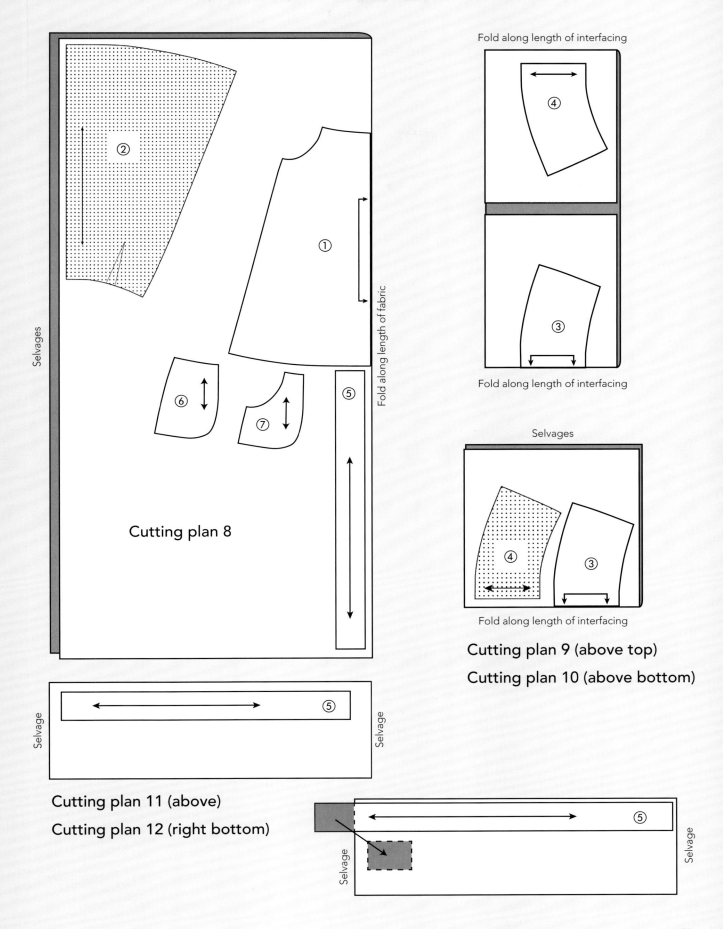

Fold along length of interfacing

④

③

Fold along length of interfacing

Selvages

④

③

Fold along length of interfacing

Cutting plan 9 (above top)

Cutting plan 10 (above bottom)

Selvages

②

①

⑥

⑦

⑤

Fold along length of fabric

Cutting plan 8

⑤

Selvage

Cutting plan 11 (above)

Cutting plan 12 (right bottom)

⑤

Selvage

Selvage

PUTTING IT TOGETHER

Seam allowance is ⅝ in. (1.5 cm)

Hem allowance is ¾ in. (2 cm)

Key to diagrams

Right side   Wrong side   Interfacing

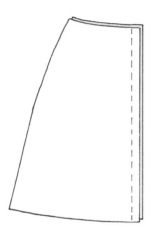

Plain with front seam version

If the version you're making has a center front seam, as in my denim skirt, join this first. With right sides together, pin the skirt fronts together along the center front seam (the center front is the straight edge without any notches). Baste (tack), machine the seam, and neaten the raw edges (see Seams, page 136).

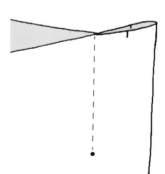

Center front pleat version

1 Bring the two outer pleat lines on the skirt front together so that they line up, with the right sides of the fabric together. Pin and baste down the line to the dot. On your machine, straight stitch as far as the dot, following the basting stitches and reverse stitching at each end to secure the stitching.

2 Open out the skirt and flatten the tuck of fabric that has been formed so that the line you've just machined is level with the middle of the tuck. Baste across the top of the pleat to hold it in place while you put the rest of the skirt together.

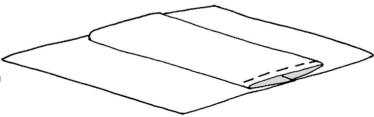

Pocket version

Attach the upper pocket bags to the skirt front and make the pockets (see Pockets—Front Hip or Cut-away, page 154).

All versions: stitching darts, staystitching, inserting zipper, stitching side seams

1 Stitch the darts in the skirt backs (see Darts, page 142).

STAYSTITCHING

Staystitching is a single line of machine straight stitch through a single layer of fabric (you're not joining anything), just inside the seam line (so if the seam allowance is ⅝ in./1.5 cm, position your staystitching at approx. ½ in./1.3 cm).

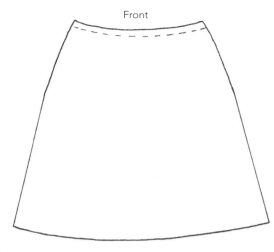

Front

Back

2 Staystitch the waist edge of the skirt front and skirt backs. This helps to stop the curved edges from stretching out of shape.

3 Insert either a centered or an invisible zipper in the center back of the skirt (see Zippers, page 143). If this is your first zipper, choose a centered, not an invisible, zipper.

4 Place the skirt front and skirt back right sides together and pin the side seams, make sure that the notches at the hipline match. Pin each end of each seam first, then match the notches, and finally pin the rest. (This seam crosses the bias in the fabric, meaning that one side can stretch easily if you start pinning at one end of the seam, resulting in mis-matched seams by the time you get to the other end.) Baste the side seams securely. Try the skirt on for size, taking care not to stretch the waist edge. Pin any adjustments, baste, and try the skirt on again to check. When you're happy with the fit, machine stitch the side seams (see Seams, page 136).

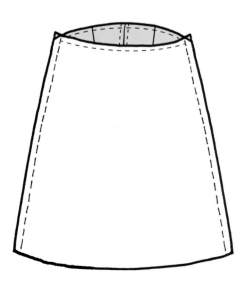

Key to diagrams

 Right side   Wrong side   Interfacing

All versions: finishing the waist with a waist facing

1 Trim ¼ in. (5 mm) from the waist facing pieces that you cut out in interfacing so that they are a bit smaller than the fabric pieces. Following the manufacturer's instructions, attach the interfacing pieces to the wrong side of the fabric waist facings. Use a muslin pressing cloth to protect your iron and fabric.

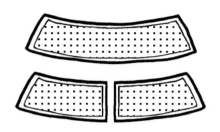

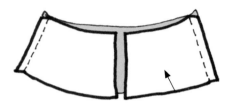

Zig-zag this edge

2 Place the front and back waist facings right sides together and pin them together at the side seams, matching the notches. Machine the seams (see Seams, page 136) and neaten all the way around the lower edge of the facings with zig-zag stitch.

3 Attach the facing to the waist of the skirt (see Attaching Waist Facings, page 146).

TIPS

Reverse stitch at the pockets if you have them, to reinforce the seam at what could be a point of strain.

*

Make sure you don't stretch the diagonal side seams, If they're wavy after zig-zagging, give them a press and they should flatten back again.

All versions: finishing the waist with a waistband

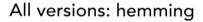

1 Trim ¼ in. (5 mm) from the waistband piece that you cut out in interfacing so that it is a bit smaller than the fabric piece. Following the manufacturer's instructions, attach the interfacing to the wrong side of the fabric waistband. Use a muslin pressing cloth to protect your iron and fabric.

2 Attach the waistband to the skirt (see Attaching Waistbands, page 147) and add the fastenings.

All versions: hemming

The hem of an A-line skirt is slightly curved. I find the best way to do them is using the Double-turned or Bias-faced Hem method (pages 139 and 140).

Topstitched version:

To add a decorative topstitch to any of your seams, see Topstitching, page 138.

FINSBURY—THE BUBBLE SKIRT

Known as a puffball skirt in the '80s, this skirt is really fun and it totally reminds me of being a schoolgirl. Even Princess Di wore one, and its varied incarnations have graced the runway shows of many a contemporary designer, including Alexander McQueen. Originally known as the "balloon" skirt by designers such as Christobal Balenciaga in the 1950s, it is Christian Lacroix who is credited with reviving "le pouf" in the '80s.

I love the sculptural quirkiness of this skirt; it's girly in an edgy kind of way and is the ideal blank canvas for showing off beautiful fabric.

Dress it up or dress it down depending what fabric you choose and how you wear it; my lightweight denim version works just as well with bare legs and sneakers in summer as it does with tights and smart shoes or boots for work in cooler months, and the multi-colored pleated hem version in silk poplin really needs nothing more than the simplest of tops and shoes to have everyone asking which designer your amazing skirt is by. I'm currently dreaming of a gorgeous crisp, black taffeta version for nights out.

You can make this skirt in a variety of lengths, with or without pockets, and with a gathered or a pleated hem.

If the sculptural bubble style is just a step too far for you, you can also use this pattern to make a simple gathered skirt. However, if you really want to go for it with a bubble skirt, do what they did in the 1950s, when some balloon skirts were stuffed with tulle to make them even bigger!

Follow the instructions in Sizing & Taking Measurements (page 130) for exactly where and how to measure yourself and how to choose which size to make.

**WITH THIS SKIRT, YOU
WILL PRACTICE THE
FOLLOWING BASIC
TECHNIQUES:**

- Seams • Hems • Pleats
- Gathering
- Attaching waistbands
- Pockets—in-seam
- Inserting invisible zippers

FINISHED SKIRT MEASUREMENTS

	34¾ in. (88 cm)	36¼ in. (92 cm)	38 in. (96 cm)	39½ in. (100 cm)	41 in. (104 cm)	43 in. (109 cm)	45 in. (114 cm)	47 in. (119 cm)	49 in. (124 cm)	51 in. (129 cm)
Size (Your actual hip measurement)										
Waist	25½ in. (65 cm)	27 in. (69 cm)	28¾ in. (73 cm)	30½ in. (77 cm)	32 in. (81 cm)	34 in. (86 cm)	36 in. (91 cm)	38 in. (96 cm)	40 in. (101 cm)	42 in. (106 cm)
Hips (measurement of hip on skirt lining of bubble versions only)	38 in. (97 cm)	40 in. (101 cm)	41½ in. (105 cm)	43 in. (109 cm)	44½ in. (113 cm)	46½ in. (118 cm)	48½ in. (123 cm)	50½ in. (128 cm)	52½ in. (133 cm)	54 ½ in. (138 cm)
Approx. length from waist seam down center back (short bubble version)	19¼ (49cm)	19¾ in. (50 cm)	20 in. (51 cm)	20½ in. (52 cm)	21 in. (53 cm)	21¼ in. (54 cm)	21¾ in. (55 cm)	22 in. (56 cm)	22½ in. (57 cm)	23 in. (58 cm)
Approx. length from waist seam down center back (knee-length bubble version)	21¾ in. (55 cm)	22 in. (56 cm)	22½ in. (57 cm)	23 in. (58 cm)	23¼ in. (59 cm)	23¾ in. (60 cm)	24 in. (61 cm)	24½ in. (62 cm)	24¾ in. (63 cm)	25¼ in. (64 cm)
Length from waist seam down center back (long gathered version)	23 in. (58 cm)	23¼ in. (59 cm)	23¾ in. (60 cm)	24 in. (61 cm)	24½ in. (62 cm)	24¾ in. (63 cm)	25¼ in. (64 cm)	25½ in. (65 cm)	26 in. (66 cm)	26¼ in. (67 cm)

WHAT FABRIC SHOULD I USE?

The bubble version works best and looks its most sculptural in crisp, light- to medium-weight woven fabrics such as silk or cotton poplin, denim, taffeta, or dupion.

The long gathered version works well in these fabrics, too, but will also look great in more fluid drapey fabrics such as rayon (viscose), cupro or silk challis, crêpe, noile, and satin.

You can choose solid colors or prints. Do not choose a knitted fabric.

My samples are made in the following fabrics:

• Knee-length blue denim bubble version with gathered hem: cotton denim

• Short multi-colored print bubble version with pleated hem: silk poplin

• Long gathered version: silk noile

If you are unsure whether a fabric is suitable, check the Fabrics Glossary (page 157).

This pattern is suitable for one-way prints and fabrics with a surface texture or pile (where the chosen size and fabric width allows).

YOU WILL NEED

For all versions

Matching sewing thread

10-in. (25-cm) zipper—an invisible zipper works best for this skirt

1 x hook and bar or button (min ⅝ in./1.5 cm diameter)

Finsbury short bubble skirt

FABRIC REQUIREMENTS

Size (Your actual hip measurement)

	34¾ in. (88 cm)	36¼ in. (92 cm)	38 in. (96 cm)	39½ in. (100 cm)	41 in. (104 cm)	43 in. (109 cm)	45 in. (114 cm)	47 in. (119 cm)	49 in. (124 cm)	51 in. (129 cm)
Outer skirt										
Fabric width										
44 in. (112 cm) or wider	2¾ yd (2.5 m)	2¾ yd (2.5 m)	2¾ yd (2.5 m)	2¾ yd (2.5 m)	2¾ yd (2.5 m)	2¾ yd (2.5 m)	2¾ yd (2.5 m)	2¾ yd (2.5 m)	2¾ yd (2.5 m)	2¾ yd (2.5 m)
55 in. (140 cm) or wider	2¾ yd (2.5 m)	2¾ yd (2.5 m)	2¾ yd (2.5 m)	2¾ yd (2.5 m)	2¾ yd (2.5 m)	2¾ yd (2.5 m)	2¾ yd (2.5 m)	2¾ yd (2.5 m)	2¾ yd (2.5 m)	2¾ yd (2.5 m)
Inner/lining skirt										
44 in. (112 cm) or wider	1⅜ yd (1.2 m)	1⅜ yd (1.2 m)	1⅜ yd (1.2 m)	1⅜ yd (1.2 m)	1⅜ yd (1.2 m)	1⅜ yd (1.2 m)	1⅜ yd (1.2 m)	1⅜ yd (1.2 m)	1⅜ yd (1.2 m)	1⅜ yd (1.2 m)
55 in. (140 cm) or wider	1 yd (0.9 m)*	1 yd (0.9 m)*	1 yd (0.9 m)*	1 yd (0.9 m)*	1 yd (0.9 m)*	1 yd (0.9 m)*	1 yd (0.9 m)*	1 yd (0.9 m)*	1 yd (0.9 m)*	1 yd (0.9 m)*
Interfacing (36 in./90 cm wide)	10 in. (25 cm)	10 in. (25 cm)	10 in. (25 cm)	10 in. (25 cm)	10 in. (25 cm)	10 in. (25 cm)	10 in. (25 cm)	10 in. (25 cm)	10 in. (25 cm)	10 in. (25 cm)

* Not suitable for fabrics that have a directional print or a pile (nap); if you are using one of these fabrics, you will need 1⅜ yd (1.2 m).

WHICH CUTTING PLAN TO FOLLOW

Outer skirt										
44 in. (112 cm) or wider	1	1	1	1	1	1	1	1	1	1
55 in. (140 cm) or wider	1	1	1	1	1	1	1	1	1	1
Inner/lining skirt										
44 in. (112 cm) or wider	2	2	2	2	2	2	2	2	2	2
55 in. (140 cm) or wider	5*	5*	5*	5*	5*	5*	5*	5*	5*	5*
Interfacing (36 in./90 cm wide)	6	6	6	6	6	7	7	7	7	7

* Only follow cutting plan 5 if you are NOT using a directional print or a fabric with a pile (nap); if you are using one of these fabrics, follow cutting plan 2.

Finsbury knee-length bubble skirt

FABRIC REQUIREMENTS

Size (Your actual hip measurement)

	34¾ in. (88 cm)	36¼ in. (92 cm)	38 in. (96 cm)	39½ in. (100 cm)	41 in. (104 cm)	43 in. (109 cm)	45 in. (114 cm)	47 in. (119 cm)	49 in. (124 cm)	51 in. (129 cm)
Outer skirt										
Fabric width 44 in. (112 cm) or wider	3 yd (2.75 m)	3 yd (2.75 m)	3 yd (2.75 m)	3 yd (2.75 m)	3 yd (2.75 m)	3 yd (2.75 m)	3 yd (2.75 m)	3 yd (2.75 m)	3 yd (2.75 m)	3 yd (2.75 m)
55 in. (140 cm) or wider	3 yd (2.75 m)	3 yd (2.75 m)	3 yd (2.75 m)	3 yd (2.75 m)	3 yd (2.75 m)	3 yd (2.75 m)	3 yd (2.75 m)	3 yd (2.75 m)	3 yd (2.75 m)	3 yd (2.75 m)
Inner/lining skirt										
44 in. (112 cm) or wider	1½ yd (1.3 m)	1½ yd (1.3 m)	1½ yd (1.3 m)	1½ yd (1.3 m)	1½ yd (1.3 m)	1½ yd (1.3 m)	1½ yd (1.3 m)	1½ yd (1.3 m)	1½ yd (1.3 m)	1½ yd (1.3 m)
55 in. (140 cm) or wider	1¼ yd (1.1 m)*	1¼ yd (1.1 m)*	1¼ yd (1.1 m)*	1¼ yd (1.1 m)*	1¼ yd (1.1 m)*	1¼ yd (1.1 m)*	1¼ yd (1.1 m)*	1¼ yd (1.1 m)*	1¼ yd (1.1 m)*	1¼ yd (1.1 m)*
Interfacing (36 in./90 cm wide)	10 in. (25 cm)	10 in. (25 cm)	10 in. (25 cm)	10 in. (25 cm)	10 in. (25 cm)	10 in. (25 cm)	10 in. (25 cm)	10 in. (25 cm)	10 in. (25 cm)	10 in. (25 cm)

* Not suitable for fabrics that have a directional print or a pile (nap); if you are using one of these fabrics, you will need 1½ yd (1.3 m).

WHICH CUTTING PLAN TO FOLLOW

	34¾ in. (88 cm)	36¼ in. (92 cm)	38 in. (96 cm)	39½ in. (100 cm)	41 in. (104 cm)	43 in. (109 cm)	45 in. (114 cm)	47 in. (119 cm)	49 in. (124 cm)	51 in. (129 cm)
Outer skirt										
44 in. (112 cm) or wider	3	3	3	3	3	3	3	3	3	3
55 in. (140 cm) or wider	4	4	4	4	4	4	4	4	4	4
Inner/lining skirt										
44 in. (112 cm) or wider	2	2	2	2	2	2	2	2	2	2
55 in. (140 cm) or wider	5*	5*	5*	5*	5*	5*	5*	5*	5*	5*
Interfacing (36 in./90 cm wide)	6	6	6	6	6	7	7	7	7	7

* Only follow cutting plan 5 if you are NOT using a directional print or a fabric with a pile (nap); if you are using one of these fabrics, follow cutting plan 2.

Finsbury long gathered skirt

FABRIC REQUIREMENTS

Size (Your actual hip measurement)

	34¾ in. (88 cm)	36¼ in. (92 cm)	38 in. (96 cm)	39½ in. (100 cm)	41 in. (104 cm)	43 in. (109 cm)	45 in. (114 cm)	47 in. (119 cm)	49 in. (124 cm)	51 in. (129 cm)
Outer skirt										
Fabric width 44 in. (112 cm) or wider	3⅜ yd (3 m)	3⅜ yd (3 m)	3⅜ yd (3 m)	3⅜ yd (3 m)	3⅜ yd (3 m)	3⅜ yd (3 m)	3⅜ yd (3 m)	3⅜ yd (3 m)	3⅜ yd (3 m)	3⅜ yd (3 m)
55 in. (140 cm) or wider	3⅜ yd (3 m)	3⅜ yd (3 m)	3⅜ yd (3 m)	3⅜ yd (3 m)	3⅜ yd (3 m)	3⅜ yd (3 m)	3⅜ yd (3 m)	3⅜ yd (3 m)	3⅜ yd (3 m)	3⅜ yd (3 m)
Inner/lining skirt										
44 in. (112 cm) or wider	1½ yd (1.35 m)	1½ yd (1.35 m)	1½ yd (1.35 m)	1½ yd (1.35 m)	1½ yd (1.35 m)	1½ yd (1.35 m)	1½ yd (1.35 m)	1½ yd (1.35 m)	1½ yd (1.35 m)	1½ yd (1.35 m)
55 in. (140 cm) or wider	1⅜ yd (1.2 m)*	1⅜ yd (1.2 m)*	1⅜ yd (1.2 m)*	1⅜ yd (1.2 m)*	1⅜ yd (1.2 m)*	1⅜ yd (1.2 m)*	1⅜ yd (1.2 m)*	1⅜ yd (1.2 m)*	1⅜ yd (1.2 m)*	1⅜ yd (1.2 m)*
Interfacing (36 in./90 cm wide)	10 in. (25 cm)	10 in. (25 cm)	10 in. (25 cm)	10 in. (25 cm)	10 in. (25 cm)	10 in. (25 cm)	10 in. (25 cm)	10 in. (25 cm)	10 in. (25 cm)	10 in. (25 cm)

* Not suitable for fabrics that have a directional print or a pile (nap); if you are using one of these fabrics, you will need 1½ yd (1.35 m).

WHICH CUTTING PLAN TO FOLLOW

	34¾ in. (88 cm)	36¼ in. (92 cm)	38 in. (96 cm)	39½ in. (100 cm)	41 in. (104 cm)	43 in. (109 cm)	45 in. (114 cm)	47 in. (119 cm)	49 in. (124 cm)	51 in. (129 cm)
Outer skirt										
44 in. (112 cm) or wider	3	3	3	3	3	3	3	3	3	3
55 in. (140 cm) or wider	4	4	4	4	4	4	4	4	4	4
Inner/lining skirt										
44 in. (112 cm) or wider	2	2	2	2	2	2	2	2	2	2
55 in. (140 cm) or wider	5*	5*	5*	5*	5*	5*	5*	5*	5*	5*
Interfacing (36 in./90 cm wide)	6	6	6	6	6	7	7	7	7	7

* Only follow cutting plan 5 if you are NOT using a directional print or a fabric with a pile (nap); if you are using one of these fabrics, follow cutting plan 2.

NOTE: I've given fabric requirements and cutting plans for all the lengths of the bubble skirt, all with pockets. If you make the outer and inner skirts from the same fabric, you need to add the fabric requirements for both skirts together; for example, to make a long gathered skirt using 55-in. (140-cm) wide fabric, you will need 4⅞ yd (4.2 m)—outer skirt (3⅜ yd/3 m) + lining skirt (1⅜ yd/1.2 m) = 4⅞ yd/4.2 m).

To make a simple gathered skirt with or without pockets, follow the fabric requirements and cutting plans for the OUTER SKIRT ONLY for the length you want to make.

PREPARING YOUR PATTERN PIECES

Trace off the pattern pieces in the size you need from the pattern sheet—bubble skirt outer front and bubble skirt outer back, bubble skirt lining front and bubble skirt lining back, waistband (use waistband pattern from Fallowfield Pencil Skirt), and pocket bags (if required) (use pocket pattern from Brighton Front-opening Skirt). To make a simple gathered skirt, you won't need the skirt lining pieces. Read the instructions in Using Paper Patterns, page 131.

CUTTING YOUR FABRIC

Make sure you read the Fabrics section (page 132) before you lay out your pattern pieces and take the scissors to your fabric!

Following the cutting plan for your fabric width and garment size, pin the pattern pieces to the fabric. Cut out all pieces in fabric, then cut out the waistband again in interfacing. Your interfacing may not be wide enough to fit the full length of the waistband pattern piece, if so, cut the waistband in 2 parts (see Cutting Plans 6 and 7). Transfer any markings to the fabric (page 133).

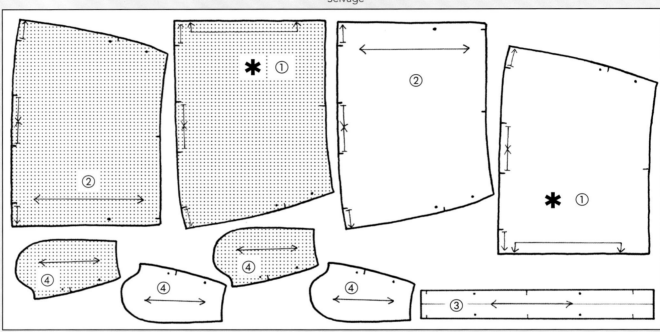

Cutting plan 1 (above)

✱ Add ⅝ in. (1.5 cm) seam allowance to center front of skirt front

Pattern pieces

① Skirt front   ④ Pocket

② Skirt back   ⑤ Lining front

③ Waistband   ⑥ Lining back

Key

Fabric

 Right side   Wrong side

Pattern pieces

Printed side up   Printed side down

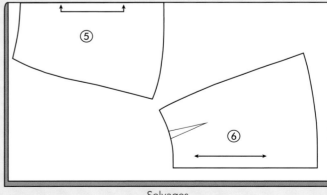

Cutting plan 2 (above)

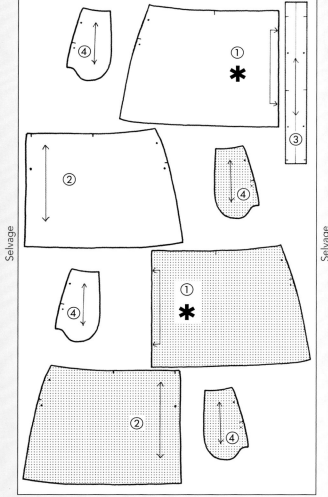

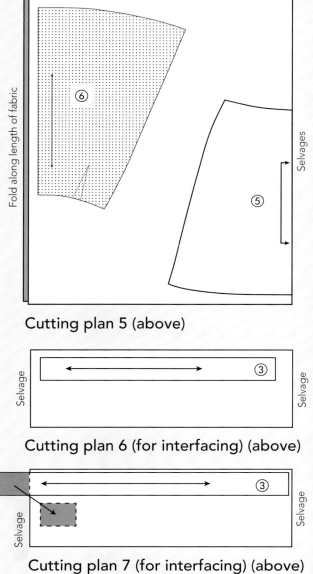

Cutting plan 3 (above)

✻ Add ⅝ in. (1.5 cm) seam allowance to center front of skirt front

Selvage

Selvage

Fold along length of fabric

Selvages

Cutting plan 4 (above)

Cutting plan 5 (above)

Cutting plan 6 (for interfacing) (above)

Cutting plan 7 (for interfacing) (above)

PUTTING IT TOGETHER

Seam allowance is ⅝ in. (1.5 cm)

Hem allowance is ¾ in. (2 cm)

Key to diagrams

Right side   Wrong side   Interfacing

All versions: stitching darts in lining, attaching optional pockets, joining side seams, staystitching lining

1 If you have used a cutting plan that told you to add a seam allowance to the center front of the outer skirt front, do this seam first. With right sides together, pin the outer skirt fronts together along the center front seam. Baste (tack), machine the seam, and neaten the raw edges (see Seams, page 136). Press the seam open.

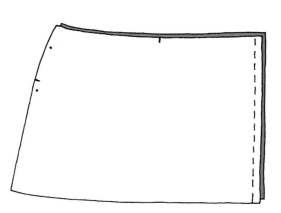

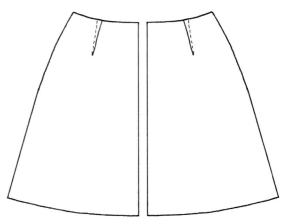

2 Stitch the darts in the lining skirt backs (see Darts, page 142).

3 If you are having in-seam pockets, you now need to attach the pocket bags. With right sides together, matching up the pocket opening dots and the notch at the hipline, pin and stitch the pockets to the side-seam edges of the outer skirt front and back pieces, making sure that the straight edge of the pocket and the straight edge of the skirt are level (see Pockets—In-Seam, page 153). NOTE: the seam allowance here is only ⅜ in. (1cm).

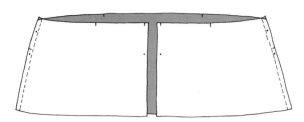

4 With right sides together, matching the single notches at the hipline, pin the outer skirt backs to the outer skirt front at the side seam (the curved edge without the dot). Pin each end of each seam first, then pin the matched notches, and finally pin the rest. (This seam crosses the bias in the fabric, meaning that one side can stretch easily if you start pinning at one end of the seam, resulting in mis-matched seams by the time you get to the other end.) Baste, machine the seam, and neaten the raw edges (see Seams, page 136). Press the seam open. If you're having in-seam pockets, see Pockets—In-Seam, page 153, for how to sew the side seams.

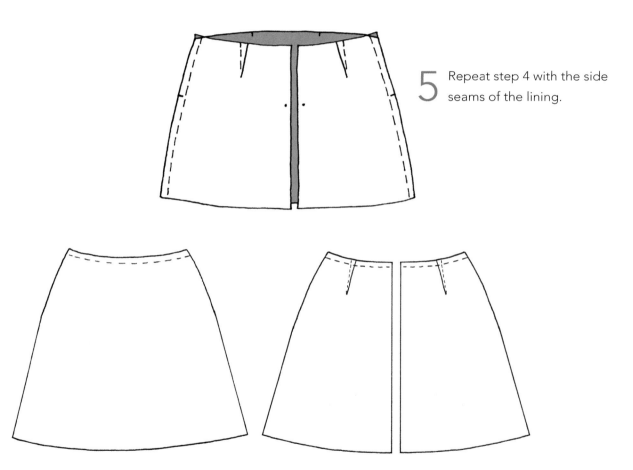

5 Repeat step 4 with the side seams of the lining.

6 Staystitch (see page 59) the waist edge of the lining skirt front and back. This helps to stop the curved edges from stretching out of shape.

7 Zig-zag the waist edges and hems of both the outer skirt and the lining skirt to neaten them and to stop the fabric from fraying and making a mess while you do the gathering.

TIP

If you're having in-seam pockets, make sure you don't catch in the tops of the pocket bags when neatening the waist of the outer skirt.

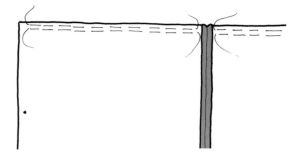

8 Machine two rows of gathering stitches along the waist edge of the outer skirt, inside the seam allowance. Machine each section of the skirt separately—start at the seam line on the back, ⅝ in. (1.5 cm) in from the center back edge, and stop just before the side seam. Do the same to the skirt front, starting just after the side seam and stopping just before the other side seam; and finally, do the same to the other skirt back, starting just after the side seam and stopping on the seam line, ⅝ in. (1.5 cm) in from the center back edge. If you are having in-seam pockets, make sure you don't catch the tops of the pocket bags in the gathering stitches. Draw up the gathering stitches until the waist of the outer skirt is the same length as the waist of the lining skirt (see Gathering, page 151).

Bubble version with gathered hem

1 Complete steps 1–8, as for all bubble versions.

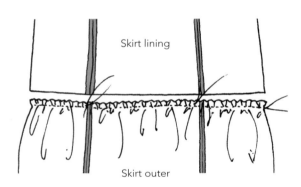

Skirt lining

Skirt outer

2 Machine two rows of gathering stitches along the hem of the outer skirt, in the same way as you did for the waist edge, and draw up the gathering stitches until the hem of the outer skirt fits the hem of the lining skirt.

3 With right sides together, matching up the side seams and notches, pin the outer and lining skirts together along the hem. Use plenty of pins, inserting them at right angles to the edge of the fabric so that you can fit more pins in and remove them easily when machining, and machine in place (see Seams, page 136). Press the seam toward the lining.

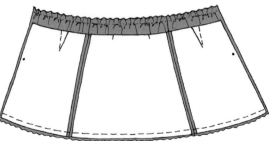

TIP

Have the lining skirt on top when machining so that the presser foot can't move the gathers.

4 Turn both outer and lining skirt layers right side out, so that the skirt can lie completely flat as a single layer of fabric.

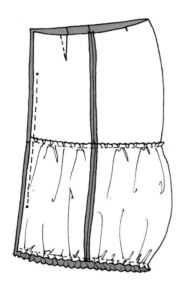

5 Fold the skirt in half along the length of the skirt, with right sides together, aligning the center back edges. Align the hem seam on either side and pin between the dots on the center back seam of the outer skirt and the center back seam of the lining skirt. Your skirt should look like a long tube, with the hem seam running around the middle. Machine between the dots only, then neaten the full length of the seam allowances of the center back edges of both the outer skirt and lining skirt (see Seams, page 136).

6 Press the seam open and insert an invisible zipper in the center back seam of the outer skirt (see Zippers, page 145).

TIP
Make sure you insert the zipper into the center back seam of the outer skirt and not the lining!

Bubble version with pleated hem

1 Complete steps 1–7, as for all bubble versions.

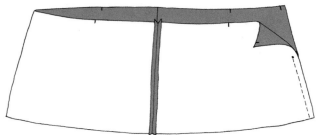

2 With right sides together, pin and stitch the center back seam of the outer skirt from the hem to the dot only. Press the seam open. Repeat with the skirt lining. Insert an invisible zipper into the center back seam of the outer skirt (see Zippers, page 145).

3 Complete step 8, as for all bubble versions, to gather the waist.

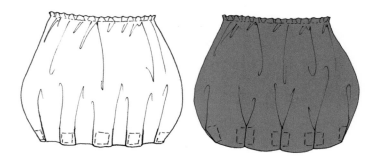

4 Instead of gathering the hem, this version uses eight inverted pleats. For each pleat bring the two outer pleat lines together so that they line up, with the right sides of the fabric together (see Pleats, page 152). Pin and baste 2 in. (5 cm) along the pleat line from the hem. Repeat with all eight pleats. (Your side seams should be in the center of two of these folds.)

5 With right sides together, matching up the side seams and the center back seams, slip the lining skirt inside the outer skirt. Pin, baste, and machine the hems together (see Seams, page 136). Press the seam toward the lining and remove the basting stitches holding the pleats in place.

All versions: attaching the lining to the zipper, attaching the waistband

1 To attach the open edges of the center back of the lining to the zipper, turn the skirt right side out, lay it flat, open the zipper, and position the center back edges of the lining level with each edge of the open zipper tape.

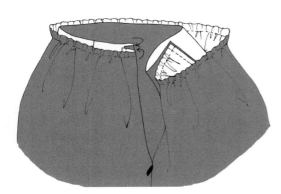

2 Working on the left-hand side of the zipper first, reach in through the open waist edge between the layers of the outer skirt and lining skirt and get hold of the left side of the open zipper and the left center back edge of the lining skirt. Bring the lining layer around so that it covers the zipper, with both layers of the skirt right sides together and the center back edges level. Pin, baste, and machine the lining to the zipper tape up to the end of the opening in the lining skirt, using a zipper foot on your sewing machine. Repeat with the right-hand side of the zipper.

3 With wrong sides together, matching the notches and side seams, pin the outer skirt to the lining skirt around the waist edge. If you have in-seam pockets, make sure the pocket bags are lying toward the front of the skirt. Machine in place inside the seam line.

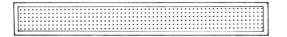

4 Trim ¼ in. (5 mm) from the waistband piece that you cut out in interfacing so that it is a bit smaller than the fabric piece. Following the manufacturer's instructions, apply the interfacing to the wrong side of the fabric waistband, using a muslin pressing cloth to protect your iron and fabric.

5 Attach the waistband to the skirt (see Attaching Waistbands, page 147) and add the fastenings.

Long gathered skirt

1 Complete steps 1, 3, and 4, as for all bubble versions.

2 Zig-zag the waist edge of the skirt to neaten it and to stop the fabric from fraying and making a mess while you do the gathering.

3 Pin the back pieces right sides together along the center back and machine from the hem to the dot only. Insert an invisible zipper into the center back seam of the outer skirt (see Zippers, page 145).

4 Trim ¼ in. (5 mm) from the waistband piece that you cut out in interfacing so that it is a bit smaller than the fabric piece. Following the manufacturer's instructions, apply the interfacing to the wrong side of the fabric waistband, using a muslin pressing cloth to protect your iron and fabric (see Applying Interfacing, page 135).

5 With the zipper open, machine two rows of gathering stitches along the waist edge of the skirt inside the seam allowance. Machine each section of the skirt separately—start just after the zipper on the center back edge and stop just before the side seam. Do the same to the skirt front, starting just after the side seam and stopping just before the other side seam. Finally, do the same to the other skirt back, starting just after the side seam and stopping just before the zipper on the center back edge. If you are having in-seam pockets, make sure you don't catch the top of the pocket bag in the gathering stitches.

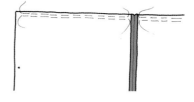

6 Draw up the gathering stitches until the waist of the outer skirt fits the waistband (see Gathering, page 151): the edges of the zipper should match the notches at the ends of the waistband (this should leave 2⅛ in./5.5 cm extending beyond the zipper at one side and only ⅝ in./1.5 cm extending beyond the other side of the zipper), the side seams of the skirt should match the dots on the waistband, and the center front of the skirt should match the remaining notch.

7 Attach the waistband to the skirt (see Attaching Waistbands, page 147) and add the fastenings.

8 The hem of this skirt is fairly straight; it just curves slightly at the side seams. Choose the best hem finish for your fabric (see Hems, page 139).

FALLOWFIELD—THE PENCIL SKIRT

A pencil skirt can be prim and proper or all-out sassy, depending on how you make it! This one is designed to sit on the natural waistline, which I find to be the most flattering for a fitted skirt.

A short denim version worn with a T-shirt can see you through the summer, or layer it up with leggings or tights and sweatshirts for winter. A lightweight wool pencil skirt makes for a smart work skirt, while cotton sateen would make a great special-occasion skirt. I keep imagining a version inspired by tuxedo trousers, using a heavy crepe for the skirt and a shiny satin for a deep waistband.

You can make the pencil skirt with a faced waist or a waistband, in three different lengths, and with a vent or godet at the back for movement in the two longer lengths. Play around with the depth of the waistband for different looks too; the standard pattern gives a waistband 1½ in. (4 cm) deep, but you could narrow it down to 1 in. (2.5 cm) or widen it up to a maximum of around 2½ in. (6 cm).

Start with a short version with a faced waist and move on to adding the godet or vent and waistband as you gain confidence.

Follow the instructions in Sizing & Taking Measurements (page 130) for exactly where and how to measure yourself and how to choose which size to make.

WITH THIS SKIRT, YOU WILL PRACTICE THE FOLLOWING BASIC TECHNIQUES:

- Seams • Hems • Vents
- Attaching waistbands
- Attaching facings
- Inserting zippers
- Inserting godets

FINISHED SKIRT MEASUREMENTS

Size (Your actual hip measurement)

	34¾ in. (88 cm)	36¼ in. (92 cm)	38 in. (96 cm)	39½ in. (100 cm)	41 in. (104 cm)	43 in. (109 cm)	45 in. (114 cm)	47 in. (119 cm)	49 in. (124 cm)	51 in. (129 cm)
Waist	25½ in. (65 cm)	27 in. (69 cm)	28¾ in. (73 cm)	30½ in. (77 cm)	32 in. (81 cm)	34 in. (86 cm)	36 in. (91 cm)	38 in. (96 cm)	40 in. (101 cm)	42 in. (106 cm)
Hips	36 in. (91 cm)	37½ in. (95 cm)	39 in. (99 cm)	40½ in. (103 cm)	42 in. (107 cm)	44 in. (112 cm)	46 in. (117 cm)	48 in. (122 cm)	50 in. (127 cm)	52 in. (132 cm)
Approx. length from waist seam down center back (short version)	16¾ in. (42.5 cm)	17 in. (43.5 cm)	17½ in. (44.5 cm)	18 in. (45.5 cm)	18½ in. (46.5 cm)	18¾ in. (47.5 cm)	19 in. (48.5 cm)	19½ in. (49.5 cm)	20 in. (50.5 cm)	20¼ in. (51.5 cm)
Approx. length from waist seam down center back (knee-length version)	22 in. (55.5 cm)	22¼ in. (56.5 cm)	22¾ in. (57.5 cm)	23 in. (58.5 cm)	23½ in. (59.5 cm)	24 in. (60.5 cm)	24¼ in. (61.5 cm)	24¾ in. (62.5 cm)	25 in. (63.5 cm)	25½ in. (64.5 cm)
Approx. length from waist seam down center back (long version)	25 in. (63.5 cm)	25½ in. (64.5 cm)	25¾ in. (65.5 cm)	26 in. (66.5 cm)	26½ in. (67.5 cm)	27 in. (68.5 cm)	27½ in. (69.5 cm)	27¾ in. (70.5 cm)	28 in. (71.5 cm)	28½ in. (72.5 cm)

WHAT FABRIC SHOULD I USE?

Pencil skirts look their best in substantial medium-weight woven fabrics such as denims, linen, cotton/linen blends, corduroy, velvet, cotton chintz, cotton poplin, lightweight wools, and stretch woven fabrics that have some elastane. This design will work well in either solid colors or prints. Do not choose a knitted fabric for this skirt.

My samples are made in the following fabrics:

- Short version with faced waist: cotton denim

- Knee-length version with vent and waistband: hand-dyed organic cotton denim

- Long version with godet and waistband: cotton/elastane denim

If you are unsure whether a fabric is suitable, check the Fabrics Glossary (page 157).

This pattern is suitable for one-way prints and fabrics with a surface texture or pile.

YOU WILL NEED

For all versions

Matching sewing thread
8-in. (20-cm) regular closed-end zipper or 9-in. (23-cm) invisible zipper (using a slightly longer invisible zipper will make it easier to insert)

For waistband version

1 x hook and bar or button (min. ⅝ in./1.5 cm diameter)

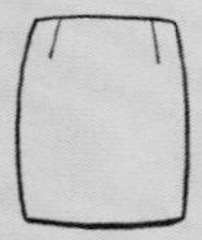

Fallowfield short version with waist facing

FABRIC REQUIREMENTS

Size (Your actual hip measurement)

Fabric width	34¾ in. (88 cm)	36¼ in. (92 cm)	38 in. (96 cm)	39½ in. (100 cm)	41 in. (104 cm)	43 in. (109 cm)	45 in. (114 cm)	47 in. (119 cm)	49 in. (124 cm)	51 in. (129 cm)
44 in. (112 cm) or wider	1¼ yd (1.1 m)	1¼ yd (1.1 m)	1¼ yd (1.1 m)	1¼ yd (1.1 m)	1¼ yd (1.1 m)	1½ yd (1.3 m)	1½ yd (1.3 m)	1½ yd (1.3 m)	1½ yd (1.3 m)	1½ yd (1.3 m)
55 in. (140 cm) or wider	¾ yd (0.7 m)	¾ yd (0.7 m)	¾ yd (0.7 m)	¾ yd (0.7 m)	¾ yd (0.7 m)	¾ yd (0.7 m)	¾ yd (0.7 m)	¾ yd (0.7 m)	¾ yd (0.7 m)	¾ yd (0.7 m)
Interfacing (36 in./90 cm wide)	10 in. (25 cm)	10 in. (25 cm)	10 in. (25 cm)	10 in. (25 cm)	10 in. (25 cm)	16 in. (40 cm)	16 in. (40 cm)	16 in. (40 cm)	16 in. (40 cm)	16 in. (40 cm)

WHICH CUTTING PLAN TO FOLLOW

Size (Your actual hip measurement)

	34¾ in. (88 cm)	36¼ in. (92 cm)	38 in. (96 cm)	39½ in. (100 cm)	41 in. (104 cm)	43 in. (109 cm)	45 in. (114 cm)	47 in. (119 cm)	49 in. (124 cm)	51 in. (129 cm)
44 in. (112 cm) or wider	2	2	2	2	2	3	3	3	3	3
55 in. (140 cm) or wider	1	1	1	1	1	1	1	1	1	1
Interfacing (36 in./90 cm wide)	4	4	4	4	4	5	5	5	5	5

Fallowfield knee-length version with waistband and back vent

FABRIC REQUIREMENTS

Size (Your actual hip measurement)

Fabric width	34¾ in. (88 cm)	36¼ in. (92 cm)	38 in. (96 cm)	39½ in. (100 cm)	41 in. (104 cm)	43 in. (109 cm)	45 in. (114 cm)	47 in. (119 cm)	49 in. (124 cm)	51 in. (129 cm)
44 in. (112 cm) or wider	1½ yd (1.4 m)	1½ yd (1.4 m)	1½ yd (1.4 m)	1½ yd (1.4 m)	1½ yd (1.4 m)	1½ yd (1.4 m)	1½ yd (1.4 m)	1½ yd (1.4 m)	1½ yd (1.4 m)	1½ yd (1.4 m)
55 in. (140 cm) or wider	1¼ yd (1.1 m)	1¼ yd (1.1 m)	1¼ yd (1.1 m)	1¼ yd (1.1 m)	1¼ yd (1.1 m)	1¼ yd (1.1 m)	1¼ yd (1.1 m)	1¼ yd (1.1 m)	1¼ yd (1.1 m)	1¼ yd (1.1 m)
Interfacing (36 in./90 cm wide)	10 in. (25 cm)	10 in. (25 cm)	10 in. (25 cm)	10 in. (25 cm)	10 in. (25 cm)	10 in. (25 cm)	10 in. (25 cm)	10 in. (25 cm)	10 in. (25 cm)	10 in. (25 cm)

WHICH CUTTING PLAN TO FOLLOW

Size (Your actual hip measurement)

	34¾ in. (88 cm)	36¼ in. (92 cm)	38 in. (96 cm)	39½ in. (100 cm)	41 in. (104 cm)	43 in. (109 cm)	45 in. (114 cm)	47 in. (119 cm)	49 in. (124 cm)	51 in. (129 cm)
44 in. (112 cm) or wider	7	7	7	7	7	7	7	7	7	7
55 in. (140 cm) or wider	6	6	6	6	6	6	6	6	6	6
Interfacing (36 in./90 cm wide)	10	10	10	10	10	11	11	11	11	11

Fallowfield long version with waistband and godet

FABRIC REQUIREMENTS

Size (Your actual hip measurement)

Fabric width	34¾ in. (88 cm)	36¼ in. (92 cm)	38 in. (96 cm)	39½ in. (100 cm)	41 in. (104 cm)	43 in. (109 cm)	45 in. (114 cm)	47 in. (119 cm)	49 in. (124 cm)	51 in. (129 cm)
44 in. (112 cm) or wider	1¾ yd (1.5 m)	1¾ yd (1.5 m)	1¾ yd (1.5 m)	1¾ yd (1.5 m)	1¾ yd (1.5 m)	1¾ yd (1.5 m)	1¾ yd (1.5 m)	1¾ yd (1.5 m)	1¾ yd (1.5 m)	1¾ yd (1.5 m)
55 in. (140 cm) or wider	1¼ yd (1.1 m)	1¼ yd (1.1 m)	1¼ yd (1.1 m)	1¼ yd (1.1 m)	1¼ yd (1.1 m)	1¼ yd (1.1 m)	1¼ yd (1.1 m)	1¼ yd (1.1 m)	1¼ yd (1.1 m)	1¼ yd (1.1 m)
Interfacing (36 in./90 cm wide)	10 in. (25 cm)	10 in. (25 cm)	10 in. (25 cm)	10 in. (25 cm)	10 in. (25 cm)	10 in. (25 cm)	10 in. (25 cm)	10 in. (25 cm)	10 in. (25 cm)	10 in. (25 cm)

WHICH CUTTING PLAN TO FOLLOW

Size (Your actual hip measurement)

	34¾ in. (88 cm)	36¼ in. (92 cm)	38 in. (96 cm)	39½ in. (100 cm)	41 in. (104 cm)	43 in. (109 cm)	45 in. (114 cm)	47 in. (119 cm)	49 in. (124 cm)	51 in. (129 cm)
44 in. (112 cm) or wider	8	8	8	8	8	8	8	8	8	8
55 in. (140 cm) or wider	9	9	9	9	9	9	9	9	9	9
Interfacing (36 in./90 cm wide)	10	10	10	10	10	11	11	11	11	11

PREPARING YOUR PATTERN PIECES

Trace off the pattern pieces in the size you need from the pattern sheet—skirt front and skirt back, front and back waist facings or waistband, and godet (if required). Read the instructions in Using Paper Patterns, page 131.

CUTTING YOUR FABRIC

Make sure you read the Fabrics section (page 132) before you lay out your pattern pieces and take the scissors to your fabric!

Following the cutting plan for your fabric width and garment size, pin the pattern pieces to the fabric. Cut out all pieces in fabric, then cut out the waist facings or waistband again in interfacing. Your interfacing may not be wide enough to fit the full length of the waistband pattern piece, if so, cut the waistband in 2 parts (see Cutting Plan 11). Transfer any markings to the fabric (page 133).

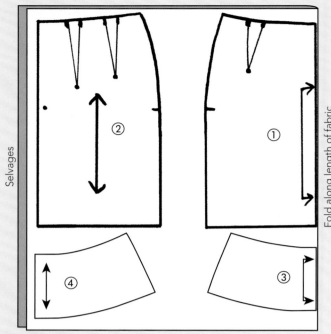

Cutting plan 1 (above)

Cutting plan 3 (below)

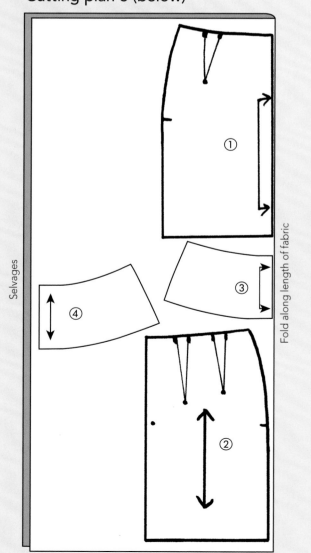

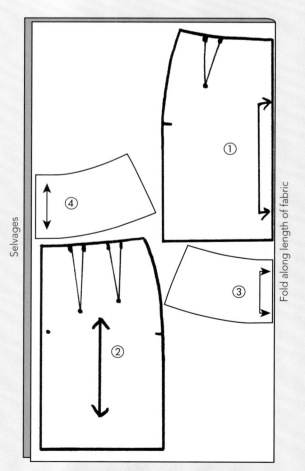

Cutting plan 2 (above)

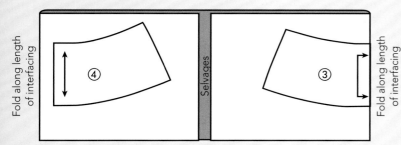

Cutting plan 4 (for interfacing) (above)

Fold along length of interfacing

Selvages

④

③

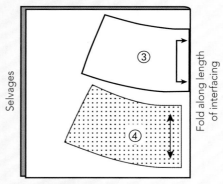

Cutting plan 5 (for interfacing) (above)

Selvages

Fold along length of interfacing

③

④

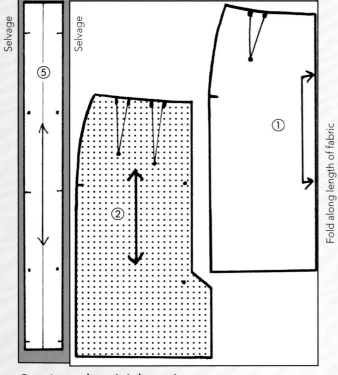

Selvage

Selvage

⑤

①

②

Fold along length of fabric

Cutting plan 6 (above)

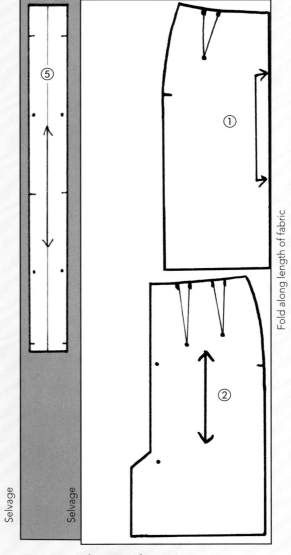

Selvage

⑤

①

②

Fold along length of fabric

Selvage

Selvage

Cutting plan 7 (above)

Pattern pieces

① Skirt front
② Skirt back
③ Front waist facing
④ Back waist facing
⑤ Waistband

Key

Fabric

Right side	Wrong side

Pattern pieces

Printed side up	Printed side down

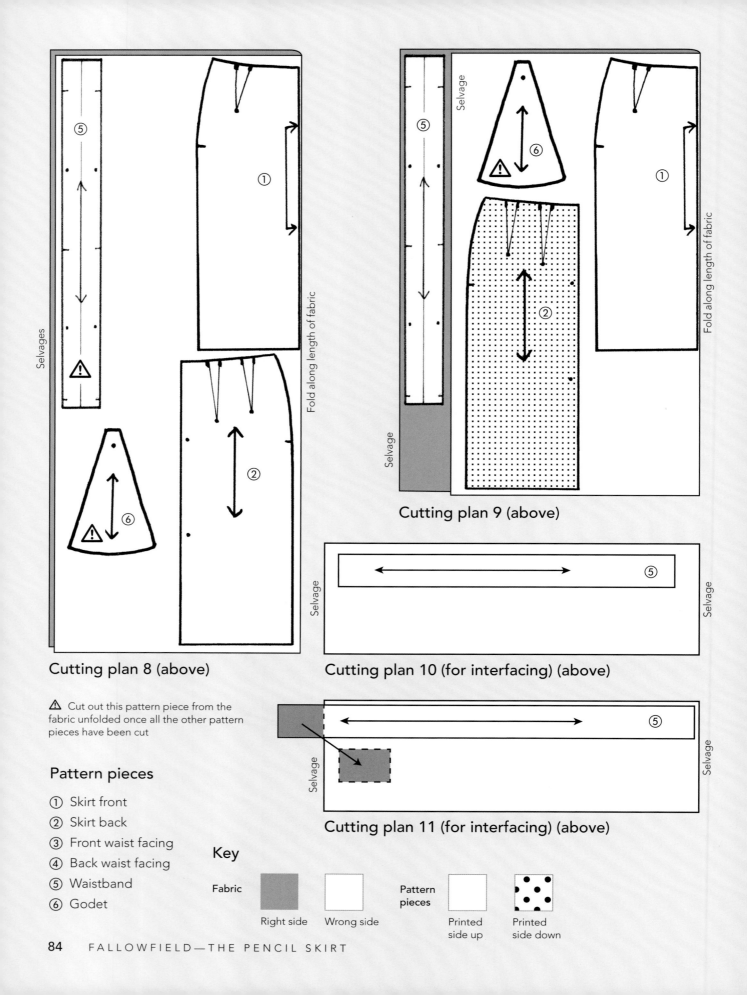

Cutting plan 8 (above)

Cutting plan 9 (above)

Cutting plan 10 (for interfacing) (above)

Cutting plan 11 (for interfacing) (above)

⚠ Cut out this pattern piece from the fabric unfolded once all the other pattern pieces have been cut

Pattern pieces

① Skirt front

② Skirt back

③ Front waist facing

④ Back waist facing

⑤ Waistband

⑥ Godet

Key

Fabric

☐ Right side ☐ Wrong side

Pattern pieces

☐ Printed side up ☐ Printed side down

PUTTING IT TOGETHER

Seam allowance is ⅝ in. (1.5 cm)
Hem allowance is ¾ in. (2 cm)

Key to diagrams

Right side

Wrong side

Interfacing

All versions: stitching darts, staystitching

1 Stitch the darts in the skirt backs and skirt front (see Darts, page 142).

2 Staystitch (page 59) the waist edge of the skirt front and skirt backs. This helps to stop the curved edges from stretching out of shape.

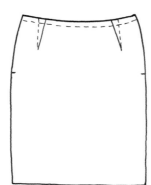

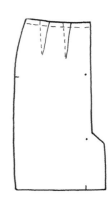

Short plain version: inserting center back zipper

1 Neaten (zig-zag) the full length of the center back seam allowances on the skirt back pieces.

2 Insert either a centered or an invisible zipper in the center back seam (see Zippers, pages 143 and 145). If this is your first zipper, choose a centered not an invisible zipper.

Knee-length version with vent: inserting center back zipper, making vent

1 Neaten (zig-zag) the full length of the center back seam allowances on the skirt backs, including across the top of the vent.

2 Neaten the long edges of the vent by either making a ¼-in. (5-mm) double-turned hem (see Hems, page 139) or finishing the edges with bias binding (see Seams—Neatening Seam Allowances, Bias Binding, page 137).

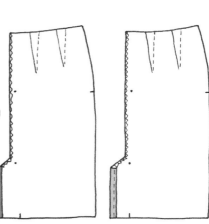

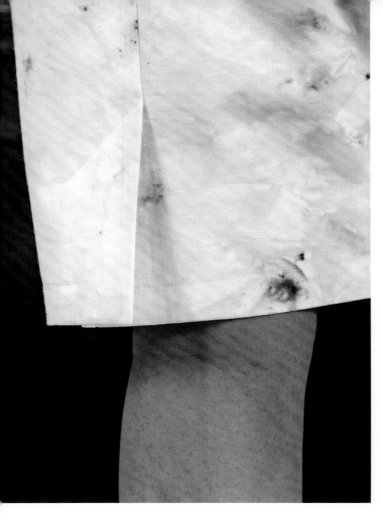

Leave open from dot to waist if using an invisible zipper

Machine stitch

3 Pin the skirt backs together along the center back seam and baste (tack) the full length of the seam.

NOTE: If you're going to use an invisible zipper, don't baste from the waist to the dot for the end of the zipper; instead, leave this part of the seam open.

4 Machine stitch between the dot for the end of the zipper and the dot for the top of the vent; at this second dot, turn and machine across the top of the vent.

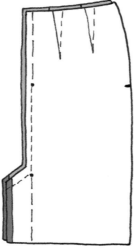

5 Press the seam open to the top of the vent and insert the zipper (see Zippers, page 143). Leave the basting stitches that are holding the vent closed in place.

TIP

If you are working with a loosely woven fabric that frays easily or a delicate fabric, place a 1¼-in. (3-cm) square of interfacing over the dot at the top of the vent on each skirt back before joining the center back seam. This will help to reinforce the top of the vent, which can be a point of strain.

---

6 With the zipper inserted and the seam pressed open as far as the vent, snip into the seam allowance of the right back skirt at the dot at the top of the vent. You will now be able to press the vent over toward the left back skirt and pin the top of the vent to the skirt.

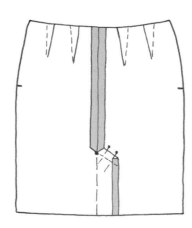

7 Following your original seam line along the top of the vent, machine stitch the vent to the skirt. Start at the dot, reverse stitch, and reverse stitch again when you reach the end of the vent. This stitching will be visible on the outside of the skirt.

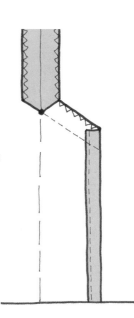

Long version with godet: inserting center back zipper and godet

1 Neaten (zig-zag) the long sides of the godet and across the top.

TIP

Remember that the long edges cross the bias of the fabric, so handle the godet gently and take care not to stretch these edges while neatening. If they are a little wavy once zig-zagged, give them a press and they should flatten down again.

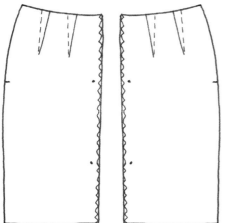

2 Neaten (zig-zag) the full length of the center back seam allowances on the skirt backs.

Leave open from dot to waist if using an invisible zipper

Machine stitch

3 Pin the skirt backs together along the center back seam and baste to the second dot only (this dot is to position the top of the godet).

NOTE: If you're going to use an invisible zipper, don't baste from the waist to the dot for the end of the zipper; instead, leave the top of the seam open and just baste between the dots.

TIP

If you are working with a loosely woven fabric that frays easily or a delicate fabric, place a 1¼-in. (3-cm) square of interfacing over the dot at the top of the godet on each skirt back before joining the center back seam. This will help to reinforce the top of the godet seam, which can be a point of strain.

4 Machine stitch between the dot for the end of the zipper and the dot for the top of the godet. Press the seam open and insert the zipper (see Zippers, page 143).

5 Lay the skirt on a flat surface, with the two backs right sides together on top of each other, and fold the top layer back out of the way from the dot that marks the top of the godet position.

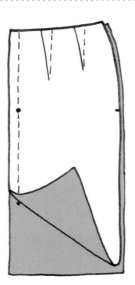

6 With right sides together, lining up the dot at the top of the godet with the dot in the center back seam, place one long edge of the godet on the exposed seam. Pin, baste securely, and machine. Make sure the stitching on this seam aligns with and meets the end of the stitching in the center back seam.

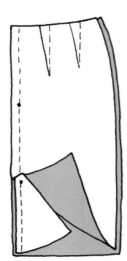

7 Pivot the godet around to join the other long edge to the other side of the center back seam. Pin and baste securely again, especially at the dot at the top of the godet, making sure you don't get any tucks at the top of the godet where the three seams meet. Once basted, turn the skirt through to the right side before machining to check that you haven't caught any tucks in the point, then machine from the dot to the hem.

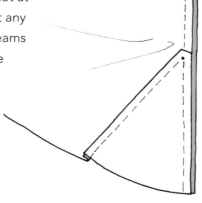

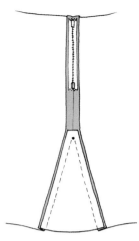

8 Press the godet seams flat, away from the godet, allowing the rest of the center back seam to stay pressed open.

All versions: stitch side seams

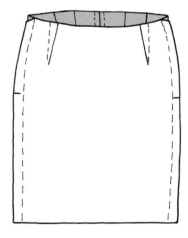

Place the skirt front and skirt back right sides together and pin the side seams, making sure that the notches at the hipline match. Pin each end of each seam first, then match the notches, and finally pin the rest. Baste the side seams securely. Try the skirt on for size, taking care not to stretch the waist edge. Pin any adjustments, baste, and try the skirt on again to check. When you're happy with the fit, machine stitch the side seams and press open (see Seams, page 136).

TIPS

If you're finishing the waist with a facing and you make an adjustment to the side seams of the skirt for fitting, you will need to make the same adjustment to the waist facing.

*

If you're finishing the waist with a waistband and bring the side seams in at the waist, you will need to remove the same amount from the waistband or it will be too big.

Finishing the waist with a waist facing

1 Trim ¼ in. (5 mm) from the waist facing pieces that you cut out in interfacing, so that they are a bit smaller than the fabric pieces. Following the manufacturer's instructions, attach the interfacing pieces to the wrong side of the fabric waist facings. Use a muslin pressing cloth to protect your iron and fabric.

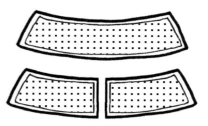

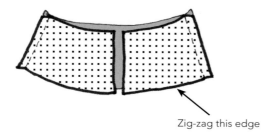

Zig-zag this edge

2 Place the front and back waist facings right sides together, matching the notches, and pin them together at the side seams. Machine the seams, press them open (see Seams, page 136), and neaten all the way around the lower edge of the facings with zig-zag stitch.

3 Attach the facing to the waist of the skirt (see Attaching Waist Facings, page 146).

Finishing the waist with a waistband

1 Trim ¼ in. (5 mm) from the waistband piece that you cut out in interfacing, so that it is a bit smaller than the fabric piece. Following the manufacturer's instructions, attach the interfacing to the wrong side of the fabric waistband. Use a muslin pressing cloth to protect your iron and fabric.

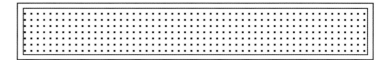

2 Attach the waistband to the skirt (see Attaching Waistbands, page 147) and add the fastening.

All versions: hemming

1 As the hem of the godet is slightly curved, you will find the Bias-faced Hem the easiest method to use for this version (see Hems, page 140).

2 The hems of the other two versions are straight, and any hemming method will work well (see page 139).

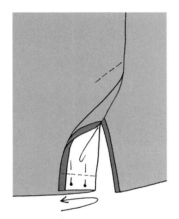

3 To finish the hem of the vented version, remove the basting stitches holding the vent closed and turn the folded back vent facing back on itself, so that the right sides of the fabric are touching. Pin in place and machine stitch the two layers together from the fold to the edge of the vent along the hemline. Remember, the hem allowance is ¾ in. (2 cm).

4 Fold the hem allowance up over the vent facing, along the stitching line you have just machined and press. This makes the corner nice and sharp when you turn the vent facing back around to the right side.

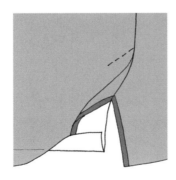

5 Continue to hem using your chosen method (see Hems, page 139).

ROEHAMPTON— THE CULOTTES

Culotte patterns are adapted from a skirt and sometimes referred to as a "divided skirt"—so that's why I've included a culotte project in your guide to skirt making!

I love culottes; practical wide-legged trousers masquerading as a flattering A-line skirt. I love the clever cutting and the optical illusion they create. If you like to travel by bicycle, you will love culottes too. In fact, if you are the kind of woman who likes to wear skirts but always finds herself with a busy life that isn't always practical in a skirt, then culottes are for you.

Culottes began to be worn by women in the early twentieth century for horse riding and were an early sign of women's emancipation, soon being adopted for riding bicycles and playing sport.

A pair of denim culottes can make a casual summer alternative to jeans with trainers or sandals and still look great with tights and boots in winter. In a longer length in fluid swishy crepe, they make a stunning alternative to an evening dress. I've given these culottes a side zipper to keep them flat fronted and to be their most flattering.

Start with the completely plain pair to get your head around the construction, have a go at the pleated version for a really luxurious feel and the optical illusion of an A-line skirt with an inverted pleat, and when you're feeling more confident try the pockets with an invisible zipper.

Follow the instructions in Sizing & Taking Measurements (page 130) for exactly where and how to measure yourself and how to choose which size to make.

WITH THIS SKIRT, YOU WILL PRACTICE THE FOLLOWING BASIC TECHNIQUES:

- Seams • Hems • Pleats
- Attaching waistbands
- Pockets—front hip/ cutaway
- Inserting zippers (lapped and invisible)

FINISHED MEASUREMENTS

Size (Your actual hip measurement)

	34¾ in. (88 cm)	36¼ in. (92 cm)	38 in. (96 cm)	39½ in. (100 cm)	41 in. (104 cm)	43 in. (109 cm)	45 in. (114 cm)	47 in. (119 cm)	49 in. (124 cm)	51 in. (129 cm)
Waist	25½ in. (65 cm)	27 in. (69 cm)	28¾ in. (73 cm)	30½ in. (77 cm)	32 in. (81 cm)	34 in. (86 cm)	36 in. (91 cm)	38 in. (96 cm)	40 in. (101 cm)	42 in. (106 cm)
Hips	40 in. (101 cm)	41½ in. (105 cm)	43 in. (109 cm)	44½ in. (113 cm)	46 in. (117 cm)	48 in. (122 cm)	50 in. (127 cm)	52 in. (132 cm)	54 in. (137 cm)	56 in. (142 cm)
Length from waist seam down outside leg / side seam (short version)	21½ in. (55 cm)	22 in. (56 cm)	22½ in. (57 cm)	23 in. (58 cm)	23¼ in. (59 cm)	23½ in. (60 cm)	24 in. (61 cm)	24½ in. (62 cm)	24¾ in. (63 cm)	25 in. (64 cm)
Length from waist seam down outside leg / side seam (knee length version)	23¼ in. (59 cm)	23½ in. (60 cm)	24 in. (61 cm)	24½ in. (62 cm)	24¾ in. (63 cm)	25 in. (64 cm)	25½ in. (65 cm)	26 in. (66 cm)	26½ in. (67 cm)	26¾ in. (68 cm)
Length from waist seam down outside leg / side seam (long version)	26½ in. (67 cm)	26¾ in. (68 cm)	27 in. (69 cm)	27½ in. (70 cm)	28 in. (71 cm)	28½ in. (72 cm)	28¾ in. (73 cm)	29 in. (74 cm)	29½ in. (75 cm)	30 in. (76 cm)

WHAT FABRIC SHOULD I USE?

Culottes work well in a wide range of medium-weight woven fabrics such as denims, linen, cotton/linen blends, corduroy, velvet, cotton chintz, cotton poplin, lightweight wools, and stretch woven fabrics that have some elastane.

Unlike the A-line skirt, culottes also work well in lighter-weight woven fabrics such as crêpe; these fabrics will create much more luxurious, dressy culottes.

You can choose solid colors or prints. Do not choose a knitted fabric.

My samples are made in the following fabrics:

• Short, plain blue denim version: cotton denim

• Knee-length cream denim version with pockets and contrast topstitching: cotton denim

• Long navy crêpe version with pleats: polyester crêpe

If you are unsure whether a fabric is suitable, check the Fabrics Glossary (page 157).

This pattern is suitable for one-way prints and fabrics with a surface texture or pile (where the chosen size and fabric width allows).

YOU WILL NEED

For all versions

Matching sewing thread

10-in. (25-cm) regular closed-end zipper or 11-in. (28-cm) invisible zipper (using a slightly longer invisible zipper will make it easier to insert) for lightweight fabrics and pocket versions

1 x hook and bar or button (min ⅝ in./1.5 cm diameter)

Roehampton short, plain version

FABRIC REQUIREMENTS

Size (Your actual hip measurement)

Fabric width	34¾ in. (88 cm)	36¼ in. (92 cm)	38 in. (96 cm)	39½ in. (100 cm)	41 in. (104 cm)	43 in. (109 cm)	45 in. (114 cm)	47 in. (119 cm)	49 in. (124 cm)	51 in. (129 cm)
44 in. (112 cm) or wider	2 yd (1.9 m)	2 yd (1.9 m)	2 yd (1.9 m)	2 yd (1.9 m)	2 yd (1.9 m)	2½ yd (2.2 m)	2½ yd (2.2 m)	2½ yd (2.2 m)	2½ yd (2.2 m)	2½ yd (2.2 m)
55 in. (140 cm) or wider	1⅞ yd (1.75 m)	1⅞ yd (1.75 m)	1⅞ yd (1.75 m)	1⅞ yd (1.75 m)	1⅞ yd (1.75 m)	1⅞ yd (1.75 m)	1⅞ yd (1.75 m)	1⅞ yd (1.75 m)	1⅞ yd (1.75 m)	1⅞ yd (1.75 m)
Interfacing (36 in./90 cm wide)	10 in. (25 cm)	10 in. (25 cm)	10 in. (25 cm)	10 in. (25 cm)	10 in. (25 cm)	10 in. (25 cm)	10 in. (25 cm)	10 in. (25 cm)	10 in. (25 cm)	10 in. (25 cm)

WHICH CUTTING PLAN TO FOLLOW

44 in. (112 cm) or wider	2	2	2	2	2	3	3	3	3	3
55 in. (140 cm) or wider	1	1	1	1	1	1	1	1	1	1
Interfacing (36 in./90 cm wide)	9	9	9	9	9	10	10	10	10	10

Roehampton knee-length version with pockets and optional topstitching

FABRIC REQUIREMENTS

Size (Your actual hip measurement)

Fabric width	34¾ in. (88 cm)	36¼ in. (92 cm)	38 in. (96 cm)	39½ in. (100 cm)	41 in. (104 cm)	43 in. (109 cm)	45 in. (114 cm)	47 in. (119 cm)	49 in. (124 cm)	51 in. (129 cm)
44 in. (112 cm) or wider	2½ yd (2.25 m)	2½ yd (2.25 m)	2½ yd (2.25 m)	2½ yd (2.25 m)	2½ yd (2.25 m)	2½ yd (2.25 m)	2½ yd (2.25 m)	2½ yd (2.25 m)	2½ yd (2.25 m)	2½ yd (2.25 m)
55 in. (140 cm) or wider	2 yd (1.9 m)	2 yd (1.9 m)	2 yd (1.9 m)	2 yd (1.9 m)	2 yd (1.9 m)	2 yd (1.9 m)	2 yd (1.9 m)	2 yd (1.9 m)	2 yd (1.9 m)	2 yd (1.9 m)
Interfacing (36 in./90 cm wide)	10 in. (25 cm)	10 in. (25 cm)	10 in. (25 cm)	10 in. (25 cm)	10 in. (25 cm)	10 in. (25 cm)	10 in. (25 cm)	10 in. (25 cm)	10 in. (25 cm)	10 in. (25 cm)

WHICH CUTTING PLAN TO FOLLOW

Size (Your actual hip measurement)

	34¾ in. (88 cm)	36¼ in. (92 cm)	38 in. (96 cm)	39½ in. (100 cm)	41 in. (104 cm)	43 in. (109 cm)	45 in. (114 cm)	47 in. (119 cm)	49 in. (124 cm)	51 in. (129 cm)
44 in. (112 cm) or wider	4	4	4	4	4	4	4	4	4	4
55 in. (140 cm) or wider	5	5	5	5	5	5	5	5	5	5
Interfacing (36 in./90 cm wide)	9	9	9	9	9	10	10	10	10	10

Roehampton long version with pleats

FABRIC REQUIREMENTS

Fabric width	Size (Your actual hip measurement)									
	34¾ in. (88 cm)	36¼ in. (92 cm)	38 in. (96 cm)	39½ in. (100 cm)	41 in. (104 cm)	43 in. (109 cm)	45 in. (114 cm)	47 in. (119 cm)	49 in. (124 cm)	51 in. (129 cm)
44 in. (112 cm) or wider	3¼ yd (3 m)	3¼ yd (3 m)	3¼ yd (3 m)	3¼ yd (3 m)	3¼ yd (3 m)	3¼ yd (3 m)	3¼ yd (3 m)	3¼ yd (3 m)	3¼ yd (3 m)	3¼ yd (3 m)
55 in. (140 cm) or wider	3 or 3¼ yd (2.75 or 3 m)*	3 or 3¼ yd (2.75 or 3 m)*	3 or 3¼ yd (2.75 or 3 m)*	3 or 3¼ yd (2.75 or 3 m)*	3 or 3¼ yd (2.75 or 3 m)*	3 or 3¼ yd (2.75 or 3 m)*	3 or 3¼ yd (2.75 or 3 m)*	3 or 3¼ yd (2.75 or 3 m)*	3 or 3¼ yd (2.75 or 3 m)*	3 or 3¼ yd (2.75 or 3 m)*
Interfacing (36 in./90 cm wide)	10 in. (25 cm)	10 in. (25 cm)	10 in. (25 cm)	10 in. (25 cm)	10 in. (25 cm)	10 in. (25 cm)	10 in. (25 cm)	10 in. (25 cm)	10 in. (25 cm)	10 in. (25 cm)

* If your fabric does not have a directional print or a pile (nap), you will need 3 yd (2.75 m); if your fabric does have a directional print or pile, you will need 3¼ yd (3 m).

WHICH CUTTING PLAN TO FOLLOW

	Size (Your actual hip measurement)									
	34¾ in. (88 cm)	36¼ in. (92 cm)	38 in. (96 cm)	39½ in. (100 cm)	41 in. (104 cm)	43 in. (109 cm)	45 in. (114 cm)	47 in. (119 cm)	49 in. (124 cm)	51 in. (129 cm)
44 in. (112 cm) or wider	6	6	6	6	6	6	6	6	6	6
55 in. (140 cm) or wider	7 or 8*	7 or 8*	7 or 8*	7 or 8*	7 or 8*	7 or 8*	7 or 8*	7 or 8*	7 or 8*	7 or 8*
Interfacing (36 in./90 cm wide)	9	9	9	9	9	10	10	10	10	10

* Only follow plan 7 if you are not using a directional print or fabric with a pile or surface texture (nap); if you are using one of these fabrics, follow cutting plan 8.

PREPARING YOUR PATTERN PIECES

Trace off the pattern pieces in the size you need from the pattern sheet—culottes front (plain or pleated) and culottes back (plain or pleated), waistband, and front facing/under pocket band and top pocket bag (if required). Read the instructions in Using Paper Patterns, page 131.

CUTTING YOUR FABRIC

Make sure you read the Fabrics section (page 132) before you lay out your pattern pieces and take the scissors to your fabric!

Following the cutting plan for your fabric width and garment size, pin the pattern pieces to the fabric. Cut out all pieces in fabric, then cut out the waistband again in interfacing. Your interfacing may not be wide enough to fit the full length of the waistband pattern piece, if so cut the waistband in 2 parts (see Cutting Plan 10). Transfer any markings to the fabric (see page 133).

Pattern pieces

① Culottes front
② Culottes back
③ Waistband
④ Front facing and under pocket
⑤ Top pocket

Key

Fabric

 Right side

 Wrong side

Pattern pieces

 Printed side up

 Printed side down

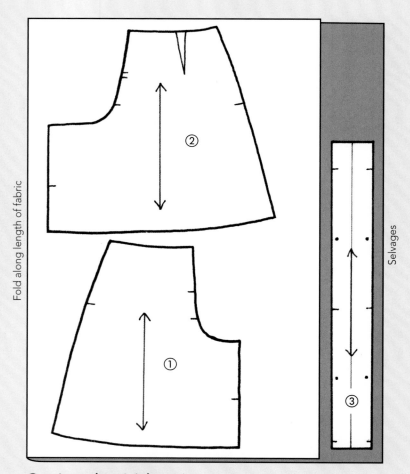

Cutting plan 1 (above)

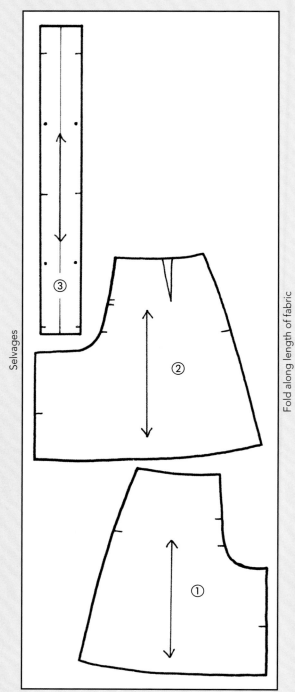

Cutting plan 2 (above)

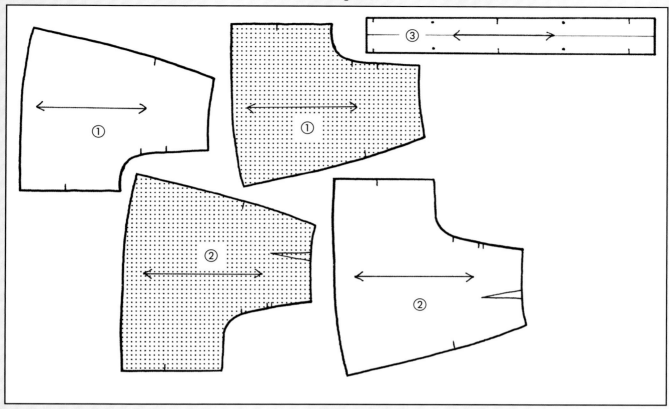

Cutting plan 3 (above)

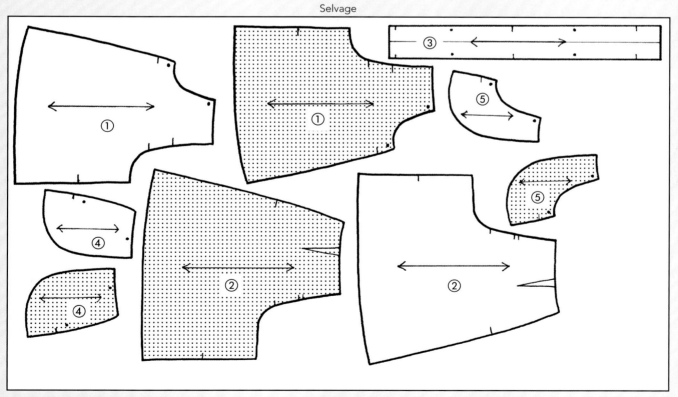

Cutting plan 4 (above)

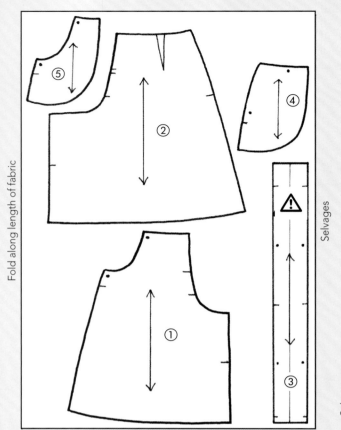

Cutting plan 5 (above)

⚠ Cut out this pattern piece from the fabric unfolded once all the other pattern pieces have been cut

Pattern pieces

① Culottes front

② Culottes back

③ Waistband

④ Front facing and under pocket

⑤ Top pocket

Key

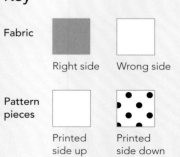

Fabric

Right side   Wrong side

Pattern pieces

Printed side up   Printed side down

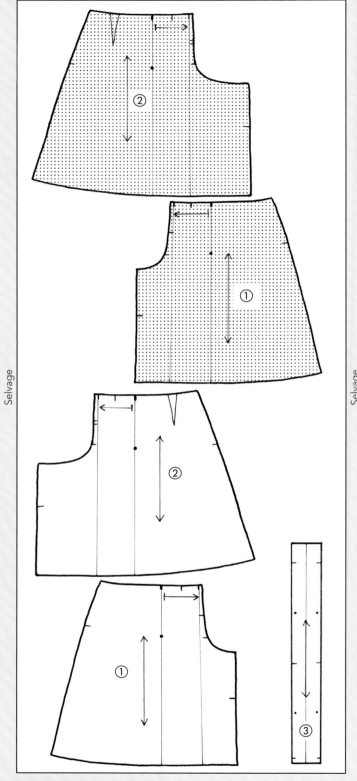

Cutting plan 6 (above)

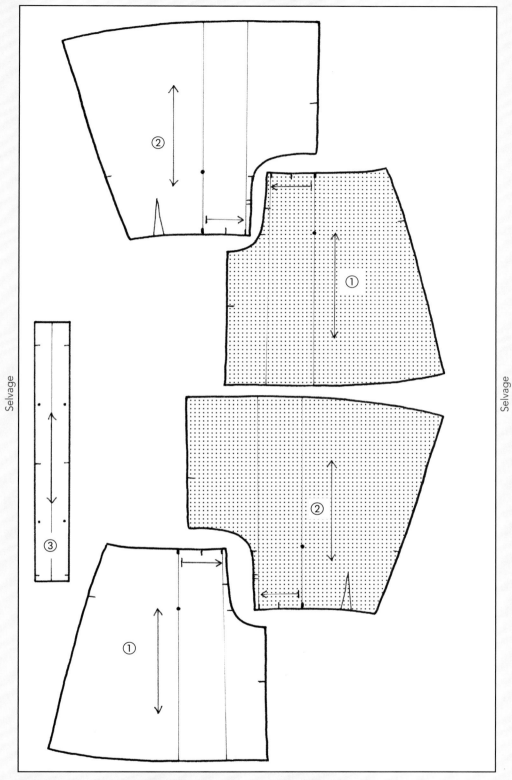

Selvage

Selvage

Cutting plan 7 (above)

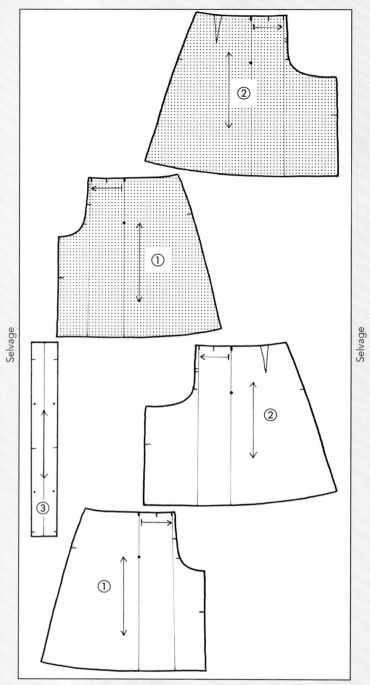

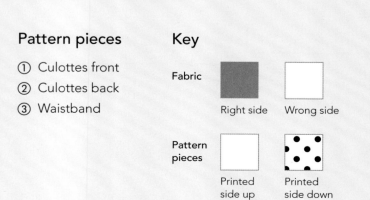

Cutting plan 8 (above)

Pattern pieces

① Culottes front
② Culottes back
③ Waistband

Key

Fabric

Right side   Wrong side

Pattern pieces

Printed side up   Printed side down

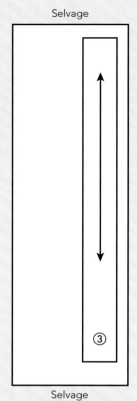

Cutting plan 9 (for interfacing)
(above)

Cutting plan 10 (for interfacing)
(above)

PUTTING IT TOGETHER

Seam allowance is ⅝ in. (1.5 cm), except for the side seams, where it is **¾ in. (2 cm)**

Hem allowance is ¾ in. (2 cm)

Key to diagrams

Right side

Wrong side

Interfacing

All versions: stitching darts, joining center front and center back seams, staystitching

1 Stitch the darts in the culotte backs (see Darts, page 142).

2 With right sides together, matching the two single notches, pin the culotte fronts together along the center front seam. Baste (tack), machine the seam, and neaten the raw edges (see Seams, page 136). Press the seam open. Repeat with the culotte backs, matching the single notch and the double notch. If you want to topstitch these seams, see Seams—Topstitching, page 138.

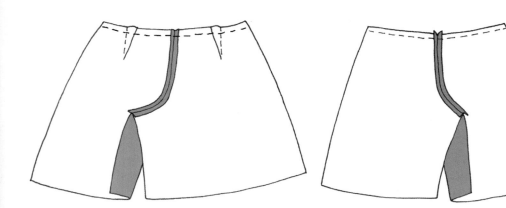

3 Staystitch (see page 59) the waist edge of the culottes front and back. This helps to stop the curved edges from stretching out of shape.

Pleated version

Bring the two outer pleat lines on the culottes front together so that they line up, with the right sides of the fabric together (see Pleats, page 152). Pin and baste (tack) the full length of the pleat line to the hem. (Your center front seam will now be in the center of this fold.) On your machine, straight stitch from the waist edge as far as the dot, following the basting stitches and reverse stitching at each end to secure the stitching. Repeat with the culottes back.

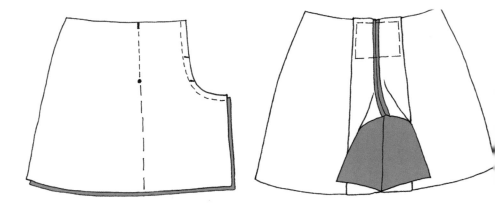

Pocket version

Matching the dots, pin the top pocket bags to the culottes front, and make the pockets (see Pockets—Front Hip/Cutaway, page 154).

All versions: inserting zipper, stitching side seams, stitching inside leg seams

(NOTE: REMEMBER—the side seams have a **¾-in./2-cm** seam allowance.)

1 Insert a zipper in the left side seam of the culottes. If you're making the version with pockets you will need to use an invisible zipper; if you're making the other two versions you can choose to use either a lapped or invisible zipper (see Zippers, page 143).

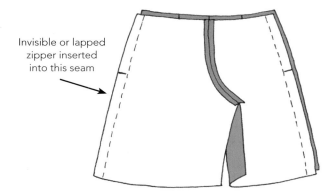

Invisible or lapped zipper inserted into this seam

2 Place the culottes front and culottes back right sides together, matching the notches at the hipline, and pin the right side seam. Pin each end of each seam first, then match the notches, and finally pin the rest. (This seam crosses the bias in the fabric, meaning that one side can stretch easily if you start pinning at one end of the seam, resulting in mis-matched seams by the time you get to the other end.) Baste the side seams securely. Try the culottes on for size, taking care not to stretch the waist edge. Pin any adjustments at the center front and center back seams rather than at the side seams; as the zipper is already in the left side seam, you would only be able to adjust the right side seam, which would make the culottes uneven. Baste, then try the culottes on again to check. When you're happy with the fit, machine stitch the right side seam, using a ¾ in. (2-cm) seam allowance (see Seams, page 136).

TIPS

Reverse stitch at the pockets, if you have them, to reinforce the seam at what could be a point of strain.

*

Make sure you don't stretch the diagonal side seams. If they're wavy after zig-zagging, give them a press and they should flatten back again.

3 To join the inside leg seams, keep the culottes inside out, place the front and back inside legs together, and pin the seam, making sure that the center front and center back seams line up and the notches match. Baste, machine the seam, and neaten the raw edges (see Seams, page 136).

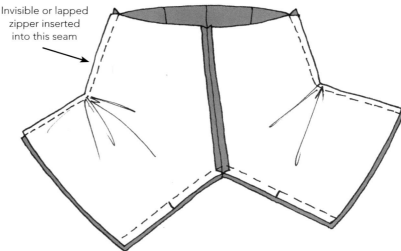

Invisible or lapped zipper inserted into this seam

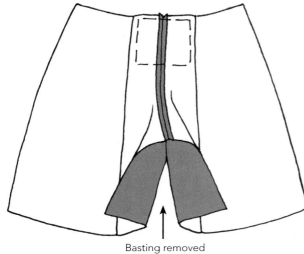

Basting removed

4 If you are making the pleated version, you will need to remove approx. 6 in. (15 cm) of the basting holding the pleats together before you can join the inside leg seams.

All versions: attaching the waistband, hemming

1 Trim ¼ in. (5 mm) from the waistband piece that you cut out in interfacing, so that it is a bit smaller than the fabric piece. Following the manufacturer's instructions, attach the interfacing to the wrong side of the fabric waistband, using a muslin pressing cloth to protect your iron and fabric.

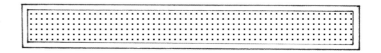

2 Attach the waistband to the culottes (see Attaching Waistbands, page 147) and add the fastening.

3 The hem of the culottes is fairly straight; it just curves slightly at the side seams. Choose the best hem finish for your fabric; I used a bias-faced hem on the plain blue denim version, a double-turned and topstitched hem on the cream version with pockets, and a neat, hand-worked blind hem on the navy crêpe pleated version (see Hems, page 139).

BRIGHTON—THE FRONT-OPENING SKIRT

Functional and really versatile, if you want to practice fastenings this is the skirt for you. It can be made with buttons, press studs, poppers, or a zipper—and, of course, you can add pockets. I can see the simple denim version worn with sneakers for summer walks with the dog or with wooly tights and boots for winter; the short zipper-front version would make a cute skirt to take on vacation; and the long button-front version is grown-up, modern girliness.

Don't be nervous about the buttons or poppers gaping, either—I've included a clever "secret" fastening at the top of the skirt, which makes sure that won't happen. If you haven't made many clothes before, try a completely plain version with press stud or popper fastenings, then have a go at pockets and buttons; if you're new to buttons and buttonholes, this is the perfect practice garment! Finally, if you think open-ended zippers must be difficult, think again: they are easier than you might imagine.

Follow the instructions in Sizing & Taking Measurements (page 130) for exactly where and how to measure yourself and how to choose which size to make.

WITH THIS SKIRT, YOU WILL PRACTICE THE FOLLOWING BASIC TECHNIQUES:

- Seams • Hems • Gathering
- Attaching waistbands
- Pockets—in-seam
- Inserting open-ended zippers
- Attaching press studs and poppers
- Making buttonholes
- Attaching buttons

FINISHED SKIRT MEASUREMENTS

Size (Your actual hip measurement)

	34¾ in. (88 cm)	36¼ in. (92 cm)	38 in. (96 cm)	39½ in. (100 cm)	41 in. (104 cm)	43 in. (109 cm)	45 in. (114 cm)	47 in. (119 cm)	49 in. (124 cm)	51 in. (129 cm)
Waist	25½ in. (65 cm)	27 in. (69 cm)	28¾ in. (73 cm)	30½ in. (77 cm)	32 in. (81 cm)	34 in. (86 cm)	36 in. (91 cm)	38 in. (96 cm)	40 in. (101 cm)	42 in. (106 cm)
Approx. length from waist seam down center back (short version)	18¼ in. (46.5 cm)	18¾ in. (47.5 cm)	19 in. (48.5 cm)	19½ in. (49.5 cm)	19¾ in. (50.5 cm)	20¼ in. (51.5 cm)	20¾ in. (52.5 cm)	21 in. (53.5 cm)	21½ in. (54.5 cm)	21¾ in. (55.5 cm)
Approx. length from waist seam down center back (knee length)	22½ in. (57 cm)	23 in. (58 cm)	23¼ in. (59 cm)	23½ in. (60 cm)	24 in. (61 cm)	24¼ in. (62 cm)	24¾ in. (63 cm)	25 in. (64 cm)	25½ in. (65 cm)	26 in. (66 cm)
Approx. length from waist seam down center back (long)	24¾ in. (62.5 cm)	25 in. (63.5 cm)	25¼ in. (64.5 cm)	25¾ in. (65.5 cm)	26¼ in. (66.5 cm)	26½ in. (67.5 cm)	27 in. (68.5 cm)	27½ in. (69.5 cm)	27¾ in. (70.5 cm)	28 in. (71.5 cm)

WHAT FABRIC SHOULD I USE?

This skirt works really well in medium-weight woven fabrics such as lightweight denims, cotton/linen blends, needlecord, cotton chintz, cotton poplin, and lightweight wools. It will work well in either solid colors or prints.

It will also look great in more fluid drapey fabrics such as rayon (viscose) poplin, cupro or silk challis, crêpe, noile, and satin.

You can choose solid colors or prints. Do not choose a knitted fabric.

My samples are made in the following fabrics:

• Knee-length blue denim version: cotton denim

• Short zipper-front version: linen/silk plain denim effect fabric

• Long button-front version with pockets: viscose poplin

If you are unsure whether a fabric is suitable, check the Fabrics Glossary (page 157).

This pattern is suitable for one-way prints and fabrics with a surface texture or pile (where the chosen size and fabric width allows).

YOU WILL NEED

For all versions

Matching sewing thread

For the press stud, popper, or button versions

6 sets of press studs or poppers or 6 buttons ⅝–1 in. (1.5–2.5 cm) in diameter (5 for the short length)
1 extra popper for the secret security fastening or 1 button ⅝ in. (1.5 cm) in diameter

For the zipper version

Short length: 20-in. (51-cm) open-ended zipper
Knee length: 24-in. (61-cm) open-ended zipper
Long length: 26-in. (66-cm) zipper

Brighton short version with zipper fastening

FABRIC REQUIREMENTS

Size (Your actual hip measurement)

Fabric width	34¾ in. (88 cm)	36¼ in. (92 cm)	38 in. (96 cm)	39½ in. (100 cm)	41 in. (104 cm)	43 in. (109 cm)	45 in. (114 cm)	47 in. (119 cm)	49 in. (124 cm)	51 in. (129 cm)
44 in. (112 cm) or wider	2⅝ yd (2.4 m)	2⅝ yd (2.4 m)	2⅝ yd (2.4 m)	2⅝ yd (2.4 m)	2⅝ yd (2.4 m)	2⅝ yd (2.4 m)	2⅝ yd (2.4 m)	2⅝ yd (2.4 m)	2⅝ yd (2.4 m)	2⅝ yd (2.4 m)
55 in. (140 cm) or wider	1¾ yd (1.6 m)	1¾ yd (1.6 m)	1¾ yd (1.6 m)	1¾ yd (1.6 m)	1¾ yd (1.6 m)	1⅜ yd (1.2 m)*	1⅜ yd (1.2 m)*	1⅜ yd (1.2 m)*	1⅜ yd (1.2 m)*	1⅜ yd (1.2 m)*
Interfacing (36 in./90 cm wide)	10 in. (25 cm)	10 in. (25 cm)	10 in. (25 cm)	10 in. (25 cm)	10 in. (25 cm)	10 in. (25 cm)	10 in. (25 cm)	10 in. (25 cm)	10 in. (25 cm)	10 in. (25 cm)

* Not suitable for directional prints or fabrics with a pile or surface texture (nap); if you are using one of these fabrics, you will need 2.4m.

WHICH CUTTING PLAN TO FOLLOW

44 in. (112 cm) or wider	9	9	9	9	9	9	9	9	9	9
55 in. (140 cm) or wider	7	7	7	7	7	8*	8*	8*	8*	8*
Interfacing (36 in./90 cm wide)	12	12	12	12	12	13	13	13	13	13

* Only follow cutting plan 8 if you are not using a directional print or a fabric with a pile (nap); if you are using one of these fabrics, follow cutting plan 9.

Brighton knee-length version with press stud, popper, or button fastening

FABRIC REQUIREMENTS

Size (Your actual hip measurement)

Fabric width	34¾ in. (88 cm)	36¼ in. (92 cm)	38 in. (96 cm)	39½ in. (100 cm)	41 in. (104 cm)	43 in. (109 cm)	45 in. (114 cm)	47 in. (119 cm)	49 in. (124 cm)	51 in. (129 cm)
44 in. (112 cm) or wider	3 yd (2.75 m)	3 yd (2.75 m)	3 yd (2.75 m)	3 yd (2.75 m)	3 yd (2.75 m)	3 yd (2.75 m)	3 yd (2.75 m)	3 yd (2.75 m)	3 yd (2.75 m)	3 yd (2.75 m)
55 in. (140 cm) or wider	2 yd (1.9 m)	2 yd (1.9 m)	2 yd (1.9 m)	2 yd (1.9 m)	2 yd (1.9 m)	2⅞ yd (2.65 m)*	2⅞ yd (2.65 m)*	2⅞ yd (2.65 m)*	2⅞ yd (2.65 m)*	2⅞ yd (2.65 m)*
Interfacing (36 in./90 cm wide)	10 in. (25 cm)	10 in. (25 cm)	10 in. (25 cm)	10 in. (25 cm)	10 in. (25 cm)	10 in. (25 cm)	10 in. (25 cm)	10 in. (25 cm)	10 in. (25 cm)	10 in. (25 cm)

* Not suitable for directional prints or fabrics with a pile or surface texture (nap); if you are using one of these fabrics, you will need 3 yd (2.8 m).

WHICH CUTTING PLAN TO FOLLOW

44 in. (112 cm) or wider	3	3	3	3	3	3	3	3	3	3
55 in. (140 cm) or wider	2	2	2	2	2	1*	1*	1*	1*	1*
Interfacing (36 in./90 cm wide)	10	10	10	10	10	11	11	11	11	11

* Only follow cutting plan 1 if you are NOT using a directional print or a fabric with a pile (nap); if you are using one of these fabrics, follow cutting plan 3.

Brighton long version with press stud, popper, or button fastening and pockets

FABRIC REQUIREMENTS

Size (Your actual hip measurement)

Fabric width	34¾ in. (88 cm)	36¼ in. (92 cm)	38 in. (96 cm)	39½ in. (100 cm)	41 in. (104 cm)	43 in. (109 cm)	45 in. (114 cm)	47 in. (119 cm)	49 in. (124 cm)	51 in. (129 cm)
44 in. (112 cm) or wider	3¼ yd (3 m)	3¼ yd (3 m)	3¼ yd (3 m)	3¼ yd (3 m)	3¼ yd (3 m)	3¼ yd (3 m)	3¼ yd (3 m)	3¼ yd (3 m)	3¼ yd (3 m)	3¼ yd (3 m)
55 in. (140 cm) or wider	2¼ yd (2.1 m)	2¼ yd (2.1 m)	2¼ yd (2.1 m)	2¼ yd (2.1 m)	3¼ yd (3 m)	3¼ yd (3 m)	3¼ yd (3 m)	3¼ yd (3 m)	3¼ yd (3 m)	3¼ yd (3 m)
Interfacing (36 in./90 cm wide)	10 in. (25 cm)	10 in. (25 cm)	10 in. (25 cm)	10 in. (25 cm)	10 in. (25 cm)	10 in. (25 cm)	10 in. (25 cm)	10 in. (25 cm)	10 in. (25 cm)	10 in. (25 cm)

WHICH CUTTING PLAN TO FOLLOW

	34¾ in. (88 cm)	36¼ in. (92 cm)	38 in. (96 cm)	39½ in. (100 cm)	41 in. (104 cm)	43 in. (109 cm)	45 in. (114 cm)	47 in. (119 cm)	49 in. (124 cm)	51 in. (129 cm)
44 in. (112 cm) or wider	6	6	6	6	6	6	6	6	6	6
55 in. (140 cm) or wider	4	4	4	4	5	5	5	5	5	5
Interfacing (36 in./90 cm wide)	10	10	10	10	10	11	11	11	11	11

PREPARING YOUR PATTERN PIECES

Trace off the pattern pieces in the size you need from the pattern sheets—skirt front, skirt back, fold-back facing interfacing, separate front facing for the zipper version, waistband, and pocket bags (if required). Read the instructions in Using Paper Patterns, page 131.

CUTTING YOUR FABRIC

Make sure you read the Fabrics section (page 132) before you lay out your pattern pieces and take the scissors to your fabric!

Following the cutting plan for your fabric width and garment size, pin the pattern pieces to the fabric. Cut out all pieces in fabric, then cut out the waistband and fold-back facing or separate front facing in interfacing. Your interfacing may not be wide enough to fit the full length of the waistband pattern piece, if so cut the waistband in 2 parts (see Cutting Plans 11 and 13). Transfer any markings to the fabric (see page 133).

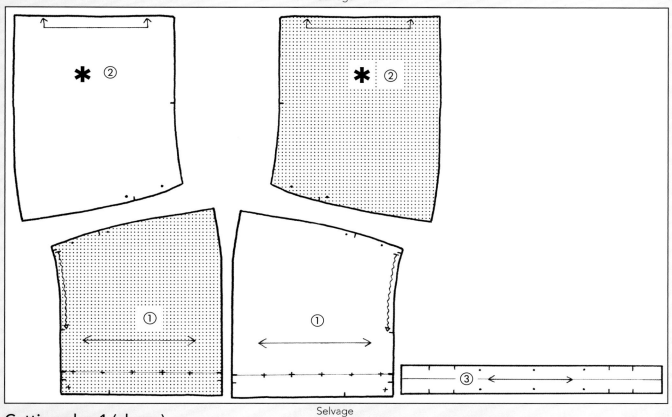

Cutting plan 1 (above)

✱ Add ⅝ in. (1.5 cm) seam allowance to center back of skirt back

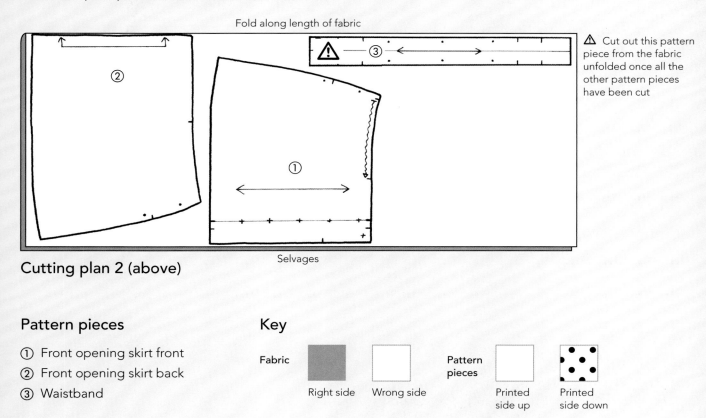

Cutting plan 2 (above)

Pattern pieces

① Front opening skirt front
② Front opening skirt back
③ Waistband

Key

Fabric			Pattern pieces		
	Right side	Wrong side		Printed side up	Printed side down

Selvage

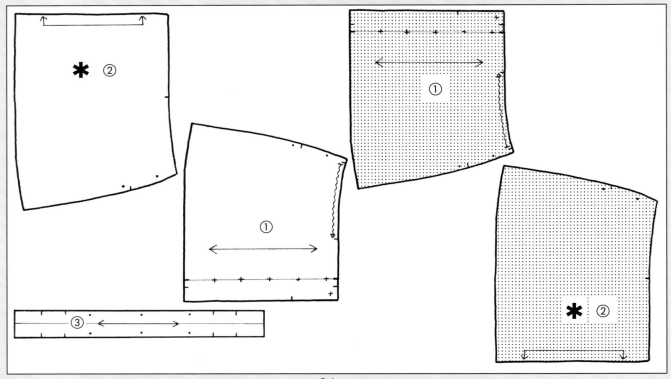

Cutting plan 3 (above)

✱ Add ⅝ in. (1.5 cm) seam allowance to center back of skirt back

Fold along length of fabric

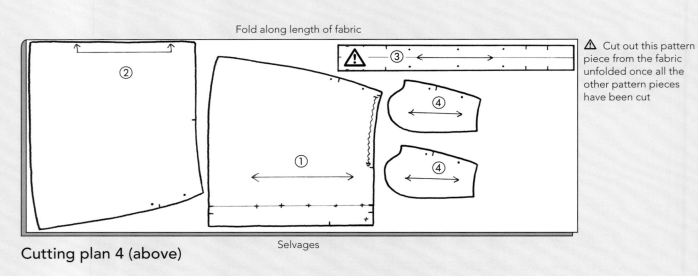

⚠ Cut out this pattern piece from the fabric unfolded once all the other pattern pieces have been cut

Selvages

Cutting plan 4 (above)

Pattern pieces

① Front opening skirt front
② Front opening skirt back
③ Waistband
④ Pocket

Key

Fabric

Right side

Wrong side

Pattern pieces

Printed side up

Printed side down

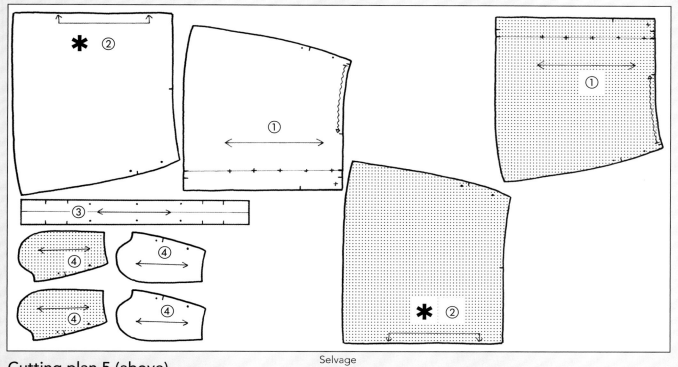

Cutting plan 5 (above)

✱ Add ⅝ in. (1.5 cm) seam allowance to center back of skirt back

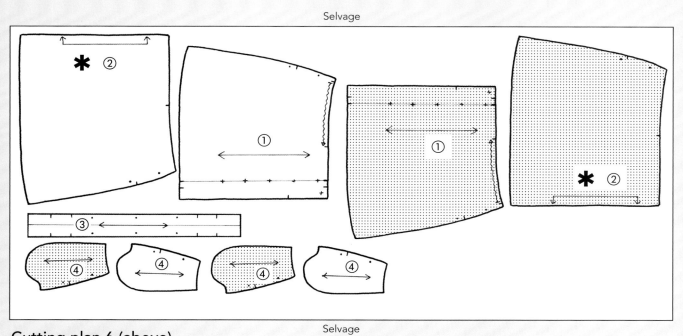

Cutting plan 6 (above)

✱ Add ⅝ in. (1.5 cm) seam allowance to center back of skirt back

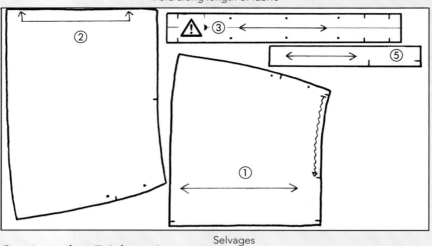

⚠ Cut out this pattern piece from the fabric unfolded once all the other pattern pieces have been cut

Selvages

Cutting plan 7 (above)

Pattern pieces

① Front opening skirt front
② Front opening skirt back
③ Waistband
④ Pocket
⑤ Separate front facing

Key

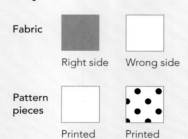

Fabric

Right side   Wrong side

Pattern pieces

Printed side up   Printed side down

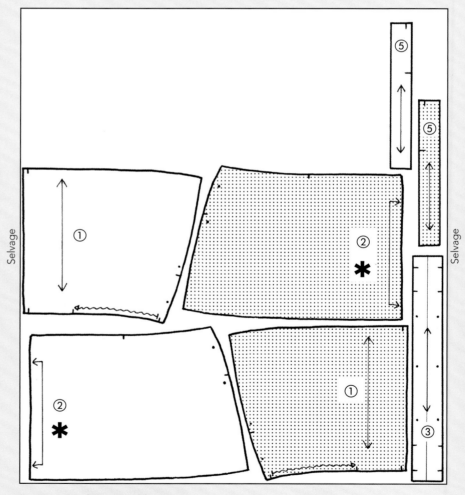

Selvage

Selvage

Cutting plan 8 (above)

✱ Add ⅝ in. (1.5 cm) seam allowance to center back of skirt back

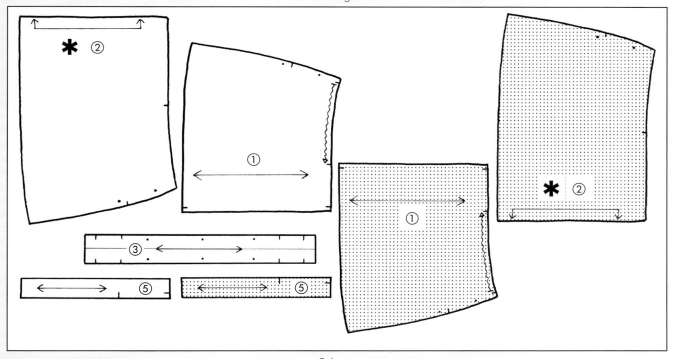

Cutting plan 9 (above)

✱ Add ⅝ in. (1.5 cm) seam allowance to center back of skirt back

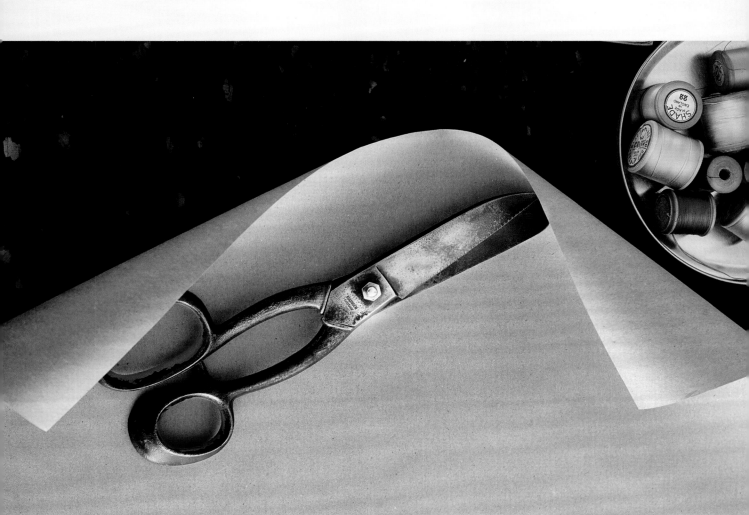

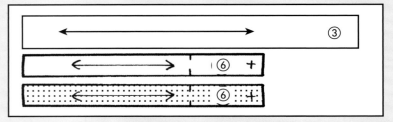

Cutting plan 10 (for interfacing) (above)

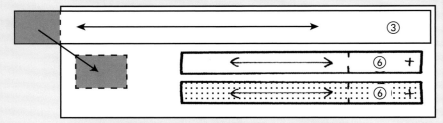

Cutting plan 11 (for interfacing) (above)

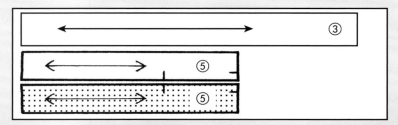

Cutting plan 12 (for interfacing) (above)

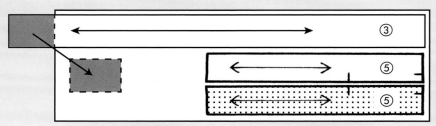

Cutting plan 13 (for interfacing) (above)

Pattern pieces

③ Waistband
⑤ Separate front facing
⑥ Fold back front interfacing

Key

Fabric	Right side	Wrong side	Pattern pieces	Printed side up	Printed side down

PUTTING IT TOGETHER

Seam allowance is ⅝ in. (1.5 cm)

Hem allowance is ¾ in. (2 cm)

Key to diagrams

Right side   Wrong side   Interfacing

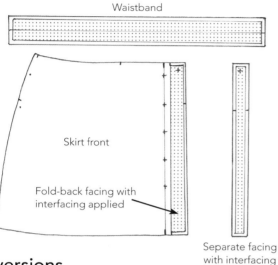

Waistband

Skirt front

Fold-back facing with interfacing applied

Separate facing with interfacing applied

All versions

Trim ¼ in. (5 mm) from the waistband piece that you cut out in interfacing, so that it is a bit smaller than the fabric waistband. Following the manufacturer's instructions, apply the interfacing to the wrong side of the fabric waistband, using a muslin pressing cloth to protect your iron and fabric. Apply the interfacing pieces to the wrong side of either the fold-back facings on the skirt fronts or to the separate front facings, depending on which version of the skirt you are making (use fold back facing for button and popper/press stud versions and use separate front facing for zipper version).

Press stud, popper, or button fastenings

1 Neaten the long, straight edges of the fold-back facing on the skirt fronts by zig-zagging the edge or attaching bias binding (see Seams—Neatening Seam Allowances, Bias Binding, page 137).

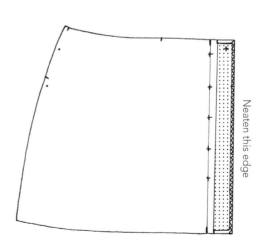

Neaten this edge

2 You will need to be able to see the center front line and the positions of fasteners on the right side of the skirt fronts and the waistband. To do this, transfer the markings from the pattern piece onto the wrong side of the fabric with chalk if you haven't already done so (see Fabrics, page 132), and then, using a contrasting thread color that will show up clearly on your fabric, baste (tack) the lines.

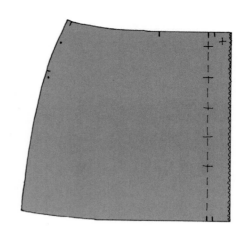

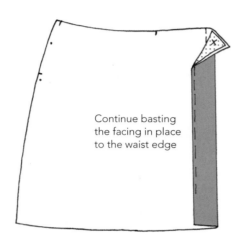

Continue basting the facing in place to the waist edge

3 Fold the facing back toward the wrong side of the fabric along the marked fold line. Press the fold and baste in place along the long loose edge, stopping approx. 4 in. (10 cm) from the hem.

4 If you have used a cutting plan that told you to add a seam allowance to the center back of the skirt back, do this seam first. With right sides together, pin the skirt backs together along the center back seam. Baste, machine the seam, and neaten the raw edges (see Seams, page 136). Press the seam open.

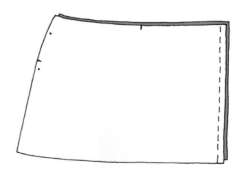

5 If you are having in-seam pockets, you now need to attach the pocket bags. With right sides together, matching up the pocket opening dots and the notch at the hipline, pin and stitch the pocket bags to the side-seam edges of the skirt front and back, making sure that the edge of the pocket and the edge of the skirt are level (see Pockets—In-Seam, page 153). NOTE: the seam allowance used here is only ⅜ in. (1 cm).

6 With right sides together, matching the single
   notches at the hipline, pin the skirt fronts to the
back at the side seams (the curved edges without the
fold-back facings). Pin each end of each seam first,
then pin the matched notches, and finally pin the rest.
(This seam crosses the bias in the fabric, meaning that
one side can stretch easily if you start pinning at one
end of the seam, resulting in mis-matched seams by
the time you get to the other end.) Baste, machine the
seam, and neaten the raw edges (see Seams, page
136). If you're having in-seam pockets, see Pockets—
In-Seam, page 153, for how to sew around the pocket
bags at the side seams.

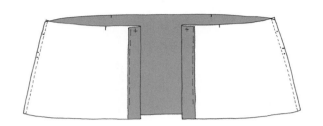

7 Zig-zag the waist edges of the skirt to neaten
   them and to stop the fabric from fraying and
making a mess while you do the gathering.

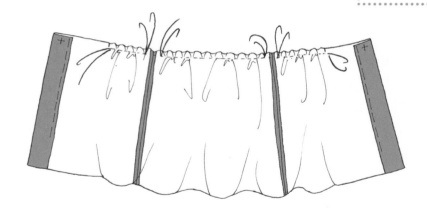

> **TIP**
>
> If you're having in-seam pockets,
> make sure you don't catch in the
> tops of the pocket bags when you
> neaten the waist.

8 Machine two rows of gathering stitches along the
   waist edge of the skirt, inside the seam allowance.
Machine each section of the skirt separately—start at
the notch on the skirt front and stop just before the
side seam. Do the same to the skirt back, starting just
after the side seam and stopping just before the other
side seam; and finally, do the same to the other skirt
front, starting just after the side seam and stopping
at the notch. If you are having in-seam pockets, make
sure you don't catch the top of the pocket bag in the
gathering stitches. Draw up the gathering stitches, but
don't secure them—we'll finalize the length in the next
step (see Gathering, page 151).

9 With right sides together, matching the center front lines in the skirt with the front notches in the waistband, and the side seams and center back in the skirt to the dots in the waistband, pin one long edge of the waistband to the skirt, so that each end of the waistband extends beyond the edge of the fold-back front facing by ⅝ in. (1.5 cm). Draw up the gathering stitches in between, so that the waist of the skirt fits the waistband, then finish the waistband (see Attaching Waistbands, page 147).

> **TIP**
>
> If you are having in-seam pockets, make sure the pockets bags are lying toward the front of the skirt when the waistband is attached.

10 Re-fold the fold-back facing at the bottom edge of the skirt the other way, so that the right sides of the fabric are together. Pin in place and machine from the folded edge to the end of the fold-back facing, ¾ in. (2 cm) above the bottom edge of the skirt.

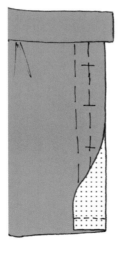

11 Turn the facing to the inside of the garment, with the wrong sides of the fabric together. To get a crisp corner at the hem, before you turn the facing, fold the seam allowance at the bottom of the facing at the start of the hem toward the wrong side of the skirt and press. When you turn the facing around, you should have a sharp corner at the center front edge of the hem.

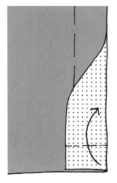

Zipper fastening

1 Neaten the two long edges of the separate front facing; it's best to zig-zag these edges (see Seams, page 137).

2 Complete steps 4–8, as for the press stud, popper, or button versions.

> **TIP**
>
> If you are having in-seam pockets, make sure the pockets bags are lying toward the front of the skirt when the waistband is attached.

3 With right sides together, matching the front notches at each end of the waistband with the notches at the front edge of the skirt, and the side and center back of the skirt to the dots in the waistband, pin one long edge of the waistband to the skirt (see Attaching Waistbands, page 147). Draw up the gathering stitches in between, so that the waist of the skirt fits the waistband. Pin the waistband in place, using lots of pins attached at right angles to the edge of the fabric to hold the gathers in place. Baste and machine the seam, with the waistband on top and the gathering on the underside so that your machine doesn't move the gathers (see Seams, page 136). Press the seam toward the waistband.

4 Separate the zipper. Place one half of the zipper right side down on the right side of the corresponding skirt front; the edge of the zipper tape should be on the same side as the edge of the fabric and the zipper teeth should be running along the seam line. The upper edge of the stopper at the top of the zipper should be touching the fold line along the center of the waistband. Pin in place.

> **TIP**
>
> Make sure the waist seam remains pressed up toward the waistband.

Fold line

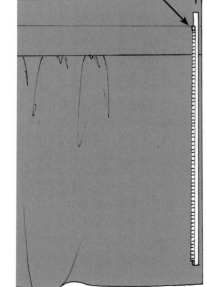

5 Before basting the zipper in place, fold over the top of the zipper tape at right angles, just above the fold line along the center of the waistband. This will give a much neater finish to the end of the zipper. Now baste the zipper in place.

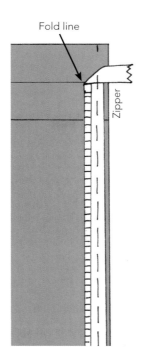

Fold line

Zipper

6 Repeat steps 4 and 5 with the other half of the zip and the other front edge of the skirt. To make sure that the waist seam will line up perfectly once the zipper is fastened, reattach the second half of the zipper to the first (now basted in place), and mark with an accurate chalk line the position of the waist seam on the second half of the zipper tape. Separate the zipper again and attach the second half in the same way as the first, making sure that your chalk mark lines up with the waist seam in the skirt.

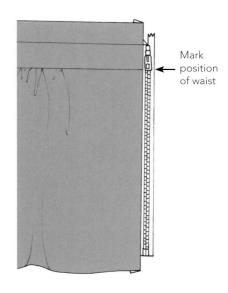

Mark position of waist

7 With right sides together, matching the notches, pin the top edge of the separate front facing to the unattached long edge of the waistband and machine in place. Press the seam toward the waistband. Repeat on the other front edge with the second separate front facing piece.

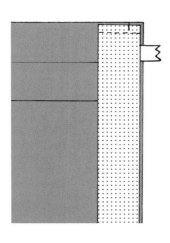

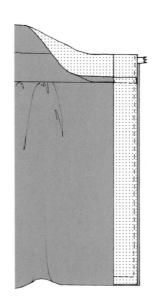

8 With right sides together, fold the waistband along the fold line so that the waistband and front facing cover the zipper and the waist seams of the waistband/skirt and the waistband/front facing are level. Pin and baste the facing in place over the zipper; the facing should reach the hem of the skirt. Baste along the long front edge and across the bottom of the facing to start forming the hem of the skirt. (Remember, the hem allowance along the bottom edge is ¾ in./2 cm.)

TIP

If it's possible on your machine, move your needle position to the far left. This allows you to sew close enough to the zipper teeth but leave enough room for the zipper foot to get around the stopper at the bottom of the zipper and the zipper pull.

9 Machine this seam using the zipper foot on your machine. Don't sew too close to the zipper teeth, as the fabric will get caught in the zipper when the skirt is worn.

10 When you start machining this seam, have the zipper pull halfway along the zipper. When you get to the zipper pull, stop sewing with the needle down in the fabric and lift up the presser foot to slide the zipper pull away from you so that you can continue sewing; if you try to sew around it, you'll get an ugly bump in your seam.

TIP

Some metal zippers have quite chunky zipper pulls and you might not be able to maneuver the zipper pull past the zipper foot. If this is the case, do a reverse stitch and remove the skirt from the machine, slide the zipper pull out of the way, and put your skirt back under the machine to continue where you left off, with another reverse stitch to secure the join in your stitching.

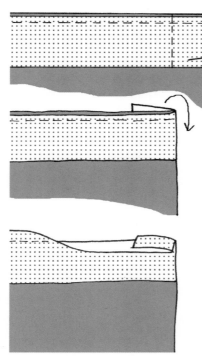

11 To get a crisp corner at the hem, before you turn the facing to the right side, fold the seam allowance along the bottom of the facing (at the start of the hemline) toward the skirt and the seam allowance along the front edge of the skirt toward the facing and press. Turn the facing to the inside of the skirt: you should have a sharp corner at the center front edge of the hem.

12 Press the skirt and facing away from the zipper. Using the zipper foot again, topstitch the seam through all the layers along the full length of the seam from the waist to the hem to prevent it from getting caught in the zipper.

13 Finish the waistband (see Attaching Waistbands, page 147).

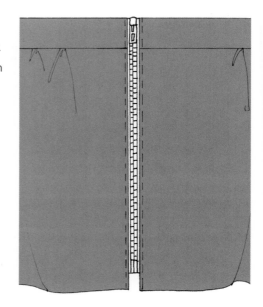

All versions: hemming

1 With your front facings turned back to the inside of the skirt , your hem will have started to fold up in the right position.

2 The hem of this skirt is fairly straight; it just curves slightly at the side seams. Choose the best hem finish for your fabric (see Hems, page 139).

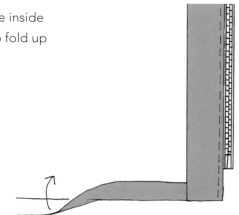

Press stud, popper, or button versions:

Attach buttons to the left front in the marked positions. Make buttonholes along the right front using your basted thread markings. If you're having press studs or poppers, attach these so that the skirt will close with the right front laying on top of the left front (see Buttons and Other Fastenings, page 150).

NOTE: make the buttonhole for the secret security fastening on the left-hand front edge through both the skirt and the fold-back facing and attach the corresponding button to the right-hand front edge. This fastening doesn't have to be a button—it could be a small snap fastener or popper. Make sure when sewing on your button/popper or attaching your press stud on the right front, you go through the facing only, not all the way through to the outside of the skirt.

TECHNIQUES: TOOLS & EQUIPMENT

You don't need a huge amount of equipment and fancy tools to make great-looking clothes. Just make sure you choose quality over quantity, gradually collect a good range of basic tools, and don't be tempted by cheap offers and the myriad "time-saving" gadgets. Most of them will just gather dust on a shelf or get lost in the bottom of a drawer.

Keep one of my favorite sayings in mind as a deterrent: "All the gear and no idea." This is not what you're aiming for!

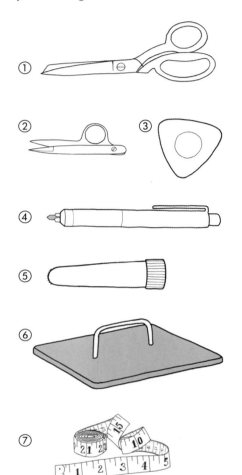

TOOLS FOR PREPARING AND CUTTING YOUR FABRIC

Scissors You will need at least three pairs. Unless you spend all of your sewing time working with slippery, lightweight fabrics, I am not a fan of cutting fabric for dressmaking with a rotary cutter.

① **Fabric scissors** Specialist fabric/dressmaking/tailor's scissors and shears have angled handles, which lets you keep the blades close to the cutting surface with the minimum lifting of your fabric. Long blades will speed up your cutting; blades at least 8 in. (20 cm) long are best. Never use your fabric scissors to cut anything but fabric if you want them to stay nice and sharp. If they do start to get a bit blunt, ask your hairdresser where they get their scissors sharpened and take yours to the same place.

General-purpose scissors You need a separate pair of scissors for cutting out paper patterns. Again, a pair with angled handles and long blades make this job easier.

② **Thread-cutting scissors or snips** A small pair of scissors with a very sharp point will be useful to keep by your sewing machine for cutting threads and for removing basting (tacking) stitches. Specialist thread snips are also useful for this job and are specially shaped to fit inside your hand, giving you maximum control over the cutting.

Marking tools Different fabrics need different types of marking tools.

③ **Tailor's chalk** The most basic way to mark fabric is with a lump of tailor's chalk. It marks well on most fabrics, but can become blunt quite quickly. They can easily be sharpened by running a scissor blade along each side of the blunt edge a few times or by using a special chalk-sharpening gadget.

④ **Chalk mechanical pencil** Easier to use than lumps of tailor's chalk and with a sharper point for more accurate marking.

⑤ **Chaco liner** These work on most fabrics and are particularly good for knitted fabrics, which can drag with pencils and tailor's chalk. They are filled with chalk dust, which brushes off easily, but you can get a very fine line.

⑥ **Weights** Use weights to hold your pattern pieces in place before pinning them onto your fabric. You don't have to use specialist ones: cans of food or paperweights work just as well.

Pattern paper Specialist dressmaker's pattern paper is strong, but thin enough to trace through and often sold from a roll by the yard (meter) or in packs of pre-cut sheets. If you can't get hold of this, rolls of wallpaper lining paper or greaseproof paper used in cooking are cheap alternatives.

⑦ **Tape measure** I prefer a plain and simple tape measure rather than the retractable ones that come in a little case, because they are cheaper and easier to use and store and the case on the retractable ones tends to get in my way.

SEWING TOOLS

Pins I find there is a critical length with pins; too short and they're useless, too long and they just get in the way. My recommendation is no shorter than 1¼ in. (30 mm) and no longer than 1½ in. (35 mm). You can get them with a bead head or without. I don't have a preference, but some people find the bead-headed pins easier to pick up.

Magnetic pincushion This is a gadget well worth investing in. No more dropped pins and you can virtually throw a handful of pins at it and they "stick."

Machine needles Most sewing machines come with a small pack of spare needles, but get yourself some more and regularly change your machine needle to prevent

it from getting blunt, bent, or chipped, which will cause problems with your sewing. Machine needles come in different sizes, with a higher number representing a thicker needle for heavier fabric. A US size 14 (UK 90) is fine for most of the fabrics that you will use in this book.

Ballpoint or jersey needles should be used when sewing knitted fabrics. These are sized in the same way as standard needles.

Here is a guide to which needle size to use for different types of woven fabrics (if you're unsure about fabric names, refer to the Fabric Glossary on page 157):

NEEDLE SIZE	FABRIC TYPE
US 11 (UK 75)	Charmeuse, crepe, satin
US 12 (UK 80)	Dupion, lawn, sateen, taffeta, challis, chambray, noile
US 14 (UK 90)	Needlecord, corduroy, lightweight denim, poplin, quilting cotton
US 16 (UK 100)	Medium- to heavyweight denim, canvas, velvet

Hand sewing needles You need some hand sewing needles. Standard hand sewing needles are described as "sharps." They are sized differently to machine needles, with a higher number meaning a thinner needle for finer fabric.

⑧ **Needle threader** An inexpensive handy gadget. To use one, feed the small wire loop through the eye of the needle, place your thread through the loop and pull it back through the eye.

⑨ **Thimble** I must confess to being a recent convert to the humble thimble. After years of sore fingers, I now use a tailor's thimble with an open top; it goes on your middle finger and you use the front of your finger to push the needle through the fabric. It takes some getting used to (there are some great videos online demonstrating the best technique), but your fingers will thank you! Thimbles come in different sizes and the right size is essential for good technique, so buy one in a store and try a few for size.

⑩ **Unpicker** It is inevitable that, at some point, you will have to unpick something, even if it's just removing basting (tacking) stitches. Unpickers are also useful for cutting buttonholes.

⑪ **Sewing machine** Probably the most expensive bit of kit you will buy, so it's a decision that requires a lot of thought and research. "Bargain" sewing machines on sale in supermarkets in my experience (and that of my students) aren't a good buy. Do your research, ask friends, look online and, most importantly, go to a specialist sewing machine store and have a go on a few. All you need, especially on your first machine, are:
- Straight stitch
- Zig-zag stitch
- A small selection of stretch stitches
- Buttonholes
- The ability to control the stitch length and stitch width

- A "free arm" (to slip sleeves and pant legs under the needle easily)
"Nice-to-haves" are:
- A speed control
- The ability to adjust the presser foot pressure.

Thread Which thread you use depends on what you are sewing:
- Basting (tacking): Use a bright color so that you can easily see to remove it, ideally something weak that you'll be able to break without too much effort, i.e. 100% cotton thread.
- Regular machine sewing: Use only branded sewing thread on your sewing machine. It is smooth and a consistent thickness–unlike cheap, unbranded threads, which tend to be fluffy and slubby. Choose the polyester version, as it is the strongest. Using cheap unbranded threads in your machine will lead to snapped threads, tangles in your machine, and tears.
- Topstitching: Choose a thicker topstitching thread from a recognized thread brand to make your topstitching stand out.

Thread color Always unwind a bit of the thread and lay it on your fabric to choose the right color. If you can't find an exact match, go a shade darker; lighter colors tend to stand out and come to the foreground and so will be more obvious on your fabric. Darker shades recede into the background.

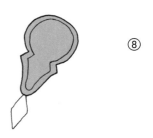

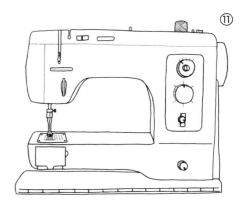

PRESSING TOOLS

Ironing board Get the biggest you can afford and have room for. Pressing is an essential part of dressmaking, and ideally you need your ironing board set up close to your sewing machine. A separate reflective ironing board cover is also a worthwhile investment, as it makes ironing quicker, won't get as dirty as a cloth cover, and adds an extra layer of padding to your board.

⑫ **Tailor's ham** So called thanks to its ham-like shape, a tailor's ham makes pressing curved seams, darts, and fiddly small areas so much easier. Once you have one you will use it almost every time you sew.

Pressing cloth A simple piece of unbleached cotton muslin is one of the cheapest and most used pieces of pressing equipment in my workshop; when placed between your fabric and your iron, it enables you to give your fabric a really good, long, hot press without the risk of scorching your fabric. It is also useful for protecting delicate fabrics when pressing and essential for protecting your iron when attaching iron-on interfacing! (See Pressing, page 135.)

⑬ **Iron** Your iron should not be too lightweight; to press well, you need weight–so a lightweight iron actually means more effort is required from you! Make sure the sole plate also has plenty of steam holes and a nice long, tapered point at the end to make it easier to iron in and around those fiddly bits of your sewing. Also look for a variable steam setting, a long cable, and a large water tank.

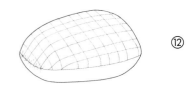

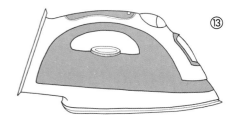

SIZING & TAKING MEASUREMENTS

Sizing is a minefield because it can tap into many women's insecurities, but you have started on your journey into making clothes that fit your body, rather than trying to make your body fit into ready-to-wear clothes. When you don't sew, the only way that many of us keep a check on our body size is by trying on clothes in stores and looking at what the size label tells us. I'm guessing that in many of the stores you go into you're a different "size" in each one. It's a practice called "vanity sizing" where retailers give different "size" labels to the same set of body measurements depending on what kind of customer they want to attract, which in my opinion makes dress sizes meaningless.

I want to be honest and totally transparent about sizing, so that's why my patterns follow the system used in men's clothing and are based on actual body measurements. All the skirts in this book have a size from 34½–51 in. (88–129 cm) and these "sizes" are the hip measurements that they will fit. Easy as that.

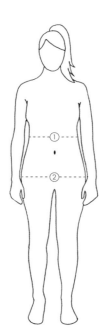

WHERE AND HOW TO MEASURE

To measure yourself you need to be standing, breathing normally (not sucking in your tummy!), and the tape measure should be snug but not tight (enough room to slide a couple of fingers underneath it). Don't measure loosely thinking that's how you'd like your garments to fit; we'll tackle that next, but for now you just need the actual dimensions of your body.

① **Waist** Tie something snugly around your middle, wriggle, and it will rest on your natural waistline. It is higher than you might have thought–just under your rib cage, well above your belly button. Measure your waist here.

② **Hips** Measure around the widest part, which is usually the biggest part of your butt, right over your hip joint. Check the tape measure in a full-length mirror to make sure it is parallel to the floor. If your widest point is lower than this, make a note of that measurement, too.

HOW TO CHOOSE WHICH SIZE TO MAKE

Here is my standard body measurement chart, which is the starting point for all the projects in this book:

	BODY MEASUREMENTS CHART
	Size (actual hip measurement)
Waist	25 in. 26¾ in. 28 in. 30 in. 31½ in. 33½ in. 35½ in. 37½ in. 39½ in. 41½ in.
	(64 cm) (68 cm) (72 cm) (76cm) (80 cm) (85 cm) (90 cm) (95 cm) (100 cm)(105 cm)
Hips	34½ in. 36 in. 37½ in. 39 in. 41 in. 43 in. 45 in. 47 in. 49 in. 51 in.
	(88 cm) (92 cm) (96 cm) (100 cm)(104 cm)(109 cm)(114 cm)(119 cm)(124 cm)(129 cm)
	Based on a standard height of 5 ft 6 in. (170 cm)

You probably won't match each measurement for a given size, because we are all different proportions. For each project, here are the measurements that you need to concentrate on matching most closely:

For these projects, choose your size based on your hip measurement:
• Roewood Jersey Pencil Skirt   • Granville Wrap Skirt   • Rusholme A-line Skirt
• Finsbury Bubble Skirt   • Fallowfield Pencil Skirt   • Roehampton Culottes
If your waist measurement differs from that given for your chosen hip measurement in the chart above, you will need to tweak the size of the waist of the pattern. See Fitting, page 155 for detailed instructions on how to adjust the patterns.

For these projects, choose your size based on your waist measurement:
• Hollings Circle Skirt (this one you draft yourself to your waist measurement)   • The simple gathered version of the Finsbury Bubble Skirt   • Brighton Front--opening Skirt
If your hip measurement differs from the one given for your chosen waist measurement in the chart above, don't worry: these skirt designs are full and very loose fitting over the hips.

TAKING EASE INTO ACCOUNT

Each project in this book has its own finished skirt measurements chart at the start of the instructions. These charts are the most crucial ones to check, as they include ease.

Ease is the difference between your body measurements and the measurements of the finished garment. Unless a garment is meant to be skin tight or stretches to fit (like the Roewood Jersey Pencil Skirt), the finished skirt measurements for a given size will always be bigger than those on the body measurements chart for that same size. How much bigger depends on:
• The amount of wearing ease (the minimum extra added for the garment to be comfortable)
• The amount of design ease (the amount added to achieve the desired fit for the design ie. a fitted versus a baggy style)
By comparing the measurements from the two size charts, you will get an idea of how loose or fitted the garment is designed to be and how it's going to fit you.

Here are two examples in size 41 in. (104 cm):

MEASUREMENT	BODY MEASUREMENTS SIZE CHART Size 41 in. (104 cm)	FINISHED SKIRT MEASUREMENTS SIZE CHART Size 41 in. (104 cm)	
		Rusholme A-line Skirt	Fallowfield Pencil Skirt
Waist	31½ in. (80 cm)	32 in. (81 cm)	32 in. (81 cm)
Hips	41 in. (104 cm)	44½ in. (113 cm)	42 in. (107 cm)

As you can see, the Rusholme A-line Skirt is a loose fit on the hips with 3½ in. (9 cm) ease and the Fallowfield Pencil Skirt is much more snug over the hips with only 1 in. (3 cm) ease.

ADJUSTING THE PATTERNS

If you are in the middle between two sizes, I recommend going up and starting with the bigger size. Try your garment on for size as soon as possible in the making process (before attaching waistbands) and simply remove any slight excess at the side seams.

All the skirts are designed to sit on the natural waistline. If you prefer your skirts to sit lower, instructions are given in Fitting on page 155.

For detailed instructions on how to adjust the patterns if your waist and hip measurements are differently proportioned to the body measurement chart, see Fitting, page 155.

USING PAPER PATTERNS

The pattern pieces for all 24 versions of the eight skirt projects in this book are printed on the three pull-out pattern sheets, no enlarging or downloading required! You will need to trace off the pattern pieces you need, though, as the patterns overlap and the pattern sheets are printed on both sides.

Here is the best way to prepare your patterns:

1 Check which pattern pieces you need to make your chosen project by reading the Preparing your Pattern Pieces section within the project instructions. NOTE–some pieces are used for more than one project.

2 Make sure you have read the Sizing & Taking Measurements section on page 130 and checked the measurement chart for the project you are making to choose the correct size.

3 Locate which pattern sheet the pieces you need are on and trace around the pieces you need in your chosen size with a highlighter pen, so that you can see them clearly.

4 Carefully trace the highlighted pattern pieces onto dressmaker's pattern paper, large sheets of tracing paper, or greaseproof paper. Make sure your paper doesn't move while tracing, as you need to be really accurate! If necessary, tape your sheets to a big table with masking tape or pin them together to stop them from moving away from each other.

5 As well as the shape of the pattern piece, also trace all the grain lines, darts, notches, placement dots, gather lines, and pleat lines that appear within that pattern piece. (See below for a full explanation of what all these symbols are for and why they are important.)

6 Some bigger pattern pieces have been printed in two or three parts, as they are too big to fit onto the pattern sheets in one piece. Where this is the case, you will see a broken "extension" line with scissors and numbered circles along the edge of the pattern where that piece ends (see above) and a corresponding extension line on the other parts of the pattern. Trace the first part of the pattern to the extension line, then align it with the extension line of the second part of the pattern (with the same numbered circles) to complete the pattern piece.

Note: All the patterns include seam and hem allowances. Seam allowances are usually 5/8 in. (1.5 cm) and hem allowances 3/4 in. (2 cm), but check the allowances given at the start of each project, as here are some that are different.

PATTERN MARKINGS

Grain lines

These lines indicate where the grain line (or lengthwise direction of the fabric) should be when that pattern piece is cut out in fabric. Most of the time the grain line runs vertically through all the different parts of your garment once it is sewn together, but there are occasions when this isn't the case (see Fabrics, page 132, for a full explanation of the grain of fabric). These marks don't need to be transferred onto your fabric; however, you do need to pay attention to them as they tell you how to position the pattern piece in relation to the straight grain in your fabric. Make sure they are parallel to the selvages (selvedges) when your pattern is pinned in place.

Place to fold line

When the grain line turns in at each end at right angles, it means that the edge of the pattern that the arrows point to needs to be placed on a lengthwise fold in the fabric. You cut around all other sides of the pattern except this one on the fold and you will end up with one big symmetrical fabric piece once the pattern is cut out.

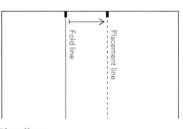

Notches

Found on the edges of patterns on seam lines, these marks are used to help you match up seams accurately and to join the right pieces together.

Placement dots

For accurate positioning of things like pockets and sometimes used as an alternative to notches where there are lots of parts to match along a seam.

Darts

Darts are large wedge shapes found on the waist of some of the skirt patterns. They shape your flat piece of fabric to fit around the curves of the body.

Gather lines

Found along the edge of a pattern piece, the wavy line indicates that this edge of the pattern piece is gathered. It is accompanied by notches or placement dots to tell you exactly where the gathering stops and starts.

Pleat lines

Pleat lines consist of a fold line and a placement line, and an arrow that tells you in which direction the fold line will lay when looked at from the right side of the fabric.

FABRICS

HOW TO CHOOSE FABRICS

One of the most common questions I'm asked by my beginner students is, "How do I know what fabric to use?" A great question–how do you know?

I've given descriptions and examples of what fabrics are best for all the skirts right at the start of each project under the heading What Fabric Should I Use? I've also made all the samples for each project in a range of fabrics to give you an idea of how different fabric choices can affect the finished look of your skirt. There is a lot more information about different kinds of fabrics and what they're best used for in the Fabric Glossary on page 157, which should be helpful if you come across a fabric and are not sure if it would be suitable. Why not make a copy of it and take it with you when you go shopping?

The next vital bits of advice I can give you on how to choose the right fabric are, I think, pretty basic, but often not even considered by beginner dressmakers.

- Look at the garments in your closet that you enjoy wearing. What colors dominate? Do you wear a lot of prints or stripes? Do you feel most comfortable in stretchy knit fabrics or structured woven fabrics? Do you mostly need warm clothes or cool ones or a balance of both?
- A novelty print may seem tempting in a fabric store, but will you really wear it? The most wearable fabrics can look a little boring when they're beside brightly colored and patterned fabrics, but don't be distracted.
- A good fabric store won't mind if you unroll some of the fabric to see how it hangs and so you can see how well it suits you.
- If you're shopping online, order a swatch first unless you know exactly what it is you're ordering.

FABRIC BASICS

So, we've started with the theory–now let's get a bit more technical. Fabric comes on a roll or bolt. Here is a diagram to guide you.

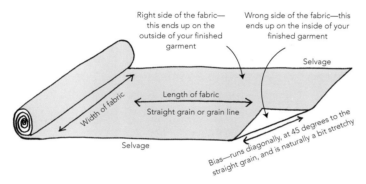

Right side of the fabric—this ends up on the outside of your finished garment

Wrong side of the fabric—this ends up on the inside of your finished garment

Selvage

Length of fabric

Straight grain or grain line

Width of fabric

Selvage

Bias—runs diagonally, at 45 degrees to the straight grain, and is naturally a bit stretchy

Fabric rolls and bolts come in a few standard different widths, from narrow quilting cottons at 44 in. (112 cm) through to knits that can be 60 in. (152 cm) or even wider.

Types of fabric

Woven fabric A stable fabric that won't stretch (unless it contains elastane). It is formed from two sets of yarns: warp threads that run along the length or grain of the fabric, and weft threads that run from side to side across the width, weaving under and over the warp threads.

Examples of woven fabrics include denim and poplin.

Knitted fabric A more flexible fabric that stretches mainly across its width. It is formed from interlocking loops of yarn. The lengthwise columns of loops are ribs; the crosswise rows are courses.

Examples of knitted fabrics include jersey (T-shirt fabric) and sweatshirt fabric.

Directional (one-way) print and nap (pile) All the projects state in the fabric requirements if they are suitable for directional (one-way) prints or fabrics with a nap or pile.

Directional or one-way prints are designs that can only be used one way round or they will appear upside down.

Fabrics with a nap or pile have a textured surface that looks and feels different depending which way up it is used. Velvet and corduroy are examples of pile fabrics.

PREWASHING AND SHRINKAGE

All fabrics should be labeled with the fiber composition (wool, polyester, cotton) and the recommended washing instructions. If not, remember to ask in the store before buying.

Always wash fabric before cutting. This is to remove any loose dye that might run and to allow the fabric to shrink if it's a fiber that's prone to shrinking.

Most sewing books and patterns don't take shrinkage into account in their fabric requirements. This is because the designer of the project has no idea what fabric you are going to choose for your project. The fabric requirements given in these projects are generous, but they don't allow for shrinkage. Here is a guide for how much fabrics MAY shrink to give you an idea how much extra you may need to buy:

- Synthetic fibers (e.g. polyester, nylon) shouldn't shrink at all.
- Cotton (especially knitted fabrics) is likely to shrink by up to 10%.
- Linen is likely to shrink by 5–10%.
- Viscose and rayon can shrink by up to 8%.
- Wool can shrink by as much as 15%.

Fabrics are best dried outside on the washing line, but if this isn't possible, knitted fabrics should be dried flat (to prevent them from stretching out of shape) and woven fabrics can be hung to dry.

> **TIP**
>
> Don't drape your fabrics over prominent shapes such as chair backs, as they'll stick into your fabric and stretch and distort the area draped over them. These mis-shapen parts are difficult to flatten out later.

CUTTING

It is important to follow the correct cutting plan for the width of fabric you are using and the project you are making. The cutting plans have been worked out for the best fit of the pattern pieces on the fabric. They are generous, so if you are a more experienced dressmaker and your fabric is wider than that given for the cutting plan, you might find that you can rearrange the pieces for a tighter fit and save some fabric.

1 Each project has a list of the pattern pieces you will need, entitled Preparing your Pattern Pieces. Once you have chosen the cutting plan for the width of fabric you are using, gather all your pattern pieces together. Also have a look at Using Paper Patterns, page 131.

2 Arrange your fabric as described in the cutting plan and place the pattern pieces as shown to check that they fit and that you have all the pieces you need.

3 Weight your pieces down and start pinning the pattern pieces onto the fabric. Pin the corners of the pattern pieces first, smoothing down the pieces so that they are nice and flat. This bit is easier if the patterns are held in place with weights. Make sure the grain lines on the pattern pieces are parallel to the selvages and that any pieces that are meant to be cut on the fold are right on the folded edge of the fabric.

4 When all your pattern pieces are in position and loosely pinned in the corners, add more pins so that the pattern pieces are securely held to the fabric, especially around any curves.

5 Now you're ready to cut. Try to have the paper pattern on the outside of your scissor blades (i.e. if you are right handed, have the pattern to the right of your scissors and if you are left handed, have the pattern to the left of your scissors). The edge of the pattern won't move as much if you cut this way. Cut as close to the paper pattern as you can without cutting through it!

6 Try not to lift up the fabric while you are cutting; keep it flat on the table and don't move it around the table. If you have enough space, move yourself around the table rather than the fabric!

TRANSFERRING PATTERN MARKINGS

Once you have cut out all the pattern pieces from your fabric, you need to transfer the pattern markings that will help you to sew the garment together onto your fabric. Most of the cutting plans tell you to pin your pattern to the wrong side of the fabric; this is the side of the fabric where we will put all the pattern markings, so that they are not visible on the outside of your garment when it's finished.

1 These are the markings that you need to transfer from the paper pattern onto your fabric with tailor's chalk or a fabric marker pen (see Tools & Equipment, page 128, for different fabric marking tools). See Using Paper Patterns, page 131, for a full explanation of what all these symbols mean.

2 Make sure you are accurate and mark them in the same position as they appear on the paper pattern; you will need to lift up the paper pattern to mark them, but don't completely unpin the pattern as it will move around and you won't then be able to transfer the markings accurately.

3 If your pattern piece was cut out through two layers of fabric, you will need to transfer the pattern markings onto both pieces of fabric. Make sure you mark the wrong side of both pieces of fabric.

WORKING WITH KNITTED FABRICS

Knitted fabrics have an undeserved reputation for being "difficult," but if you take a bit of extra care they make quick, easy-to-fit, comfortable clothes. Here are a few tips:
• Patterns are designed for either stretch knit fabrics or non-stretch woven fabrics–the two are generally not interchangeable. All projects state if they're for knitted fabrics or not.
• Knitted fabrics don't crease as much as woven fabrics.
• They have more of a tendency to shrink, especially if made from cotton.
• Knitted fabric won't fray but it will unravel slightly–some edges can be left unfinished.
• I show you some specific machine settings for sewing seams and hems in knitted fabrics using just your regular sewing machine in Sewing Knitted Fabrics, page 134.

Cutting knitted fabrics Knitted fabrics also have a straight grain. Sometimes this can be identified by blobs of glue along the selvages (lots of knitted fabrics are manufactured as a tube and this is where the tube has been cut). Alternatively, look for the vertical lines in the rows of knitting–when you look closely, many knitted fabrics will look like hand knitting but on a tiny scale.

Some knitted fabrics, such as lightweight drapey silk or viscose jersey, can move a lot when cutting. Extra pins will help keep your pattern in position and using a few weights to hold your pattern in place will help.

Make sure the fabric isn't hanging off the end of your table when cutting out knits; it will stretch. If you don't have room for the whole length of fabric on your table, pile it up over the back of a chair beside the table or roll it up on the end of the table and cut out in sections.

SEWING KNITTED FABRICS

There is a myth that knitted fabrics are difficult to work with, so new sewers are often discouraged from using them. You simply need to handle these fabrics slightly differently to woven fabrics when washing and cutting, then set up your machine correctly to sew them. Make sure you read Working with Knitted Fabrics, page 133, for instructions on washing and cutting knits. Read the Fabric Glossary on page 157 for my list of the most common knitted fabrics as some are trickier to work with than others. There is only one project in this book suitable for knitted fabrics—the Roewood Jersey Pencil Skirt, page 6—and the list of recommended knitted fabrics for it are: Single jersey, Ponte Roma, Loopback sweatshirt (or French terry) or Sweater knit. If this is your first knitted fabric garment, the easiest of these to work with is Ponte Roma. It doesn't roll when cut, is quite thick, and stays put while you are cutting and sewing.

SETTING UP YOUR MACHINE AND MACHINING TECHNIQUE

The one thing you absolutely must not do when sewing knitted fabrics on a regular sewing machine (unless explicitly told to do so) is stretch the fabric while sewing. If you do this, you will create a wavy seam or hem that is almost impossible to correct after sewing. Use exactly the same technique you would to sew a woven fabric; gently guiding the fabric through the machine, allowing the machine to feed the fabric through at its own pace.

If your fabric looks stretched after going through the machine, there are two things you can do. If your machine has the facility, lower the presser foot pressure (how hard the presser foot is pressing down on the fabric). If your machine doesn't have this facility, a walking foot can be helpful.

All knits, apart from thick, heavy ones such as loopback (or brushed back) sweatshirt, heavy sweater knits, and heavy Ponte Roma, need a ballpoint or jersey needle. These needles are slightly blunt on the end so that they work their way through the gaps formed in the knitted structure of the fabric without laddering. They come in different sizes like regular sewing needles (see Tools & Equipment, page 128).

Here's a guide for which size of needle will best suit which fabric:

NEEDLE SIZE	FABRIC TYPE
US 11 (UK 70)	Very lightweight silk or viscose jersey
US 12 (UK 80)	Light T-shirt-weight cotton jersey
US 14 (UK 90)	Interlock, Ponte Roma

NOTE: If your machine starts to skip stitches your fabric is too thick for a ballpoint needle, use a regular one.

SEAMS

I strongly recommend basting (tacking) all seams in knits to prevent stretching and to ensure your seams are accurate. Due to the stretchy nature of knitted fabrics, you can't sew them on a regular straight stitch; as soon as the fabric stretched, the stitches would snap. You need to use some kind of stretch stitch setting on your sewing machine. Here are three different ways to sew stretchy seams in knitted fabrics on any machine:

Stretch straight stitch Most modern sewing machines will have one of these stitch options; your sewing machine manual may describe it as anything from a triple straight stitch to a super-stretch stitch. This stitch is ideal if you need to press the seam open to reduce bulk–for example, the seam in the waistband of the Roewood Jersey Pencil Skirt.

Overlock stitch This is another stitch that most modern sewing machines will have. It is essentially a combination of straight and zig-zag stitches. Here are a few examples. This stitch can join the seam and neaten the edges in one go. The seam has to be pressed flat to one side rather than open, so it's not suitable for bulky fabrics. It works well on most T-shirt-weight single jerseys. You can either trim off the excess seam allowance close to the stitching for a super-neat finish or leave it–it won't fray.

Simple zig-zag stitch If you have an older or very basic sewing machine it may not have any of the stitches mentioned so far, but you can still sew knit fabrics. A simple narrow zig-zag stitch will do the job. This seam can be pressed open or to one side.

HEMS

Stretch stitch settings need to be used for hems, too. In fact, for fitted garments like the Roewood Jersey Pencil that need to be able to stretch along the hem, it's even more important to use a stretch stitch here. Always baste (tack) your hems in position first–they can easily stretch and form tucks if you try to machine them pinned. When you have finished machining any hem, remove the basting stitches, then press the fold of the hem from the wrong side of the fabric to get a nice crisp edge. Here are two ways to sew stretchy hems on any sewing machine:

Three-step zig-zag stitch Most sewing machines, even many older ones, have this stitch. It is also called a "tricot" or "elastic" stitch. Set it to a medium-to-wide stitch width and a medium length. Position the stitches so that they land just on the cut edge of your turned-up hem.

Simple zig-zag stitch Some very basic sewing machines might not have a three-step zig-zag stitch, but as long as it has a basic zig-zag stitch you can still hem your knitted fabric garments. Set the zig-zag stitch to a medium-to-wide stitch width and a medium length. Position the stitches so that they land just on the cut edge of your turned-up hem.

PRESSING

Your iron and ironing board are as important as your sewing machine when dressmaking (see Tools & Equipment, page 129 for tips on choosing).

Pressing is not ironing. Ironing is about removing creases; sometimes pressing is about adding them–but in a controlled way in strategic areas. Pressing is all about setting stitching, manipulating and controlling your fabric, and creating shape. Pressing also requires a different technique to ironing: when pressing, you need to apply varying amounts of pressure and heat in small areas, whereas ironing is maintaining a constant light pressure while moving the iron over large areas.

Try and get in the habit of pressing every seam open once you have stitched it. Pressing seams open reduces bulk and creates a beautiful flat seam on both the outside and the inside of the garment.

Pressing each seam as you have stitched it not only makes any sewing that comes afterward neater (subsequent seams that cross this first one will match more accurately if your first seam is pressed flat); it is also much easier in the long run. If you sew a second seam that crosses an un-pressed one, it is much harder to get back in to try and press them both.

Always remove basting (tacking) stitches before pressing to allow the area you are pressing to lie flat. Pressing over temporary basting stitches can also sometimes leave permanent indentations in certain fabrics.

Always test your iron's temperature on a spare bit of your fabric before pressing your garment.

All seams in the projects should be pressed open unless stated otherwise in the instructions.

TIPS FOR SUCCESSFUL PRESSING:

- Always press on the wrong side of the fabric.
- Use a bit of steam to speed up and improve your pressing.
- Take care with prints—some may melt at higher temperatures.
- Synthetic fiber fabrics need to be pressed at low temperatures.
- Natural fiber fabrics can take higher temperatures. The exception is silk, which must be pressed on a low temperature.
- Sequins or metallic prints can melt under the iron.
- If you need to press the right side of the fabric, use a pressing cloth (see page 129).
- When re-pressing areas that have been interfaced use a pressing cloth, as the interfacing can still melt.
- Don't press over pins. They can leave pin holes in your fabric.
- Use a tailor's ham (see page 129) to press darts.
- Remove basting stitches before pressing.
- Press as you go for a professional rather than a home-made finish.

INTERFACING

Interfacing is applied to the wrong side of fabric in certain parts of a garment that will be put under a lot of strain or wear and tear, to add strength and to stiffen the fabric to help it keep its shape. In skirts it is most often found in waistbands, waist facings, and along any button openings.

There are fusible (that you have to iron on) and sew-in types of interfacing as well as woven and non-woven, all in different weights or thicknesses to suit a variety of fabrics and intended uses.

Fusible or iron-on interfacing is easiest to use when you first start to sew, as it is the easiest to apply. Personally I prefer woven fusible interfacing. For most of the fabrics you will use in this book a medium-weight interfacing will be suitable.

All the projects that require interfacing will tell you which pattern pieces to cut from the interfacing in the cutting plans. As detailed in the project instructions, these pieces need to be cut a little smaller than the actual pattern piece so that, when you iron the interfacing onto your fabric, the interfacing doesn't overhang the fabric and end up stuck to your ironing board. The easiest way to do this is to pin the pattern pieces to your interfacing, chalk around the pattern pieces, unpin them, and cut about ¼ in. (5 mm) inside your chalk line. It is easiest to chalk on the non-glue side of the interfacing. The glue side will feel rough and/or look shiny.

APPLYING INTERFACING

1 Make sure your fabric pieces are flat and crease free–press them if necessary. If you attach interfacing to creased fabric, the crease becomes permanent!

2 Lay the fabric on your ironing board wrong side up and carefully place the interfacing on the fabric with the glue side of the interfacing against the wrong side of the fabric.

3 Always use a cotton muslin pressing cloth (not a dish towel) when applying interfacing. It protects your iron from getting covered in melted interfacing and your fabric from being scorched. The beauty of cotton muslin is that cotton can withstand high heat, while muslin is thin and has an open weave that allows a lot of heat to pass through it.

4 Check on the selvage of the interfacing what heat setting to use on your iron. Move your iron around slowly, making sure that the center of the sole plate passes over the edges and corners of the interfacing. You don't need to press down with the iron–it's more about the length of time that the iron is against the interfacing, this is what melts and activates the glue, not pressure.

5 Check that all the edges and corners are attached before you finish.

SEAMS

I'm going to show you some tips to keep your seams neat and accurate, a selection of different ways to finish your seam allowances, and some other things you can do with seams—understitching and topstitching.

First, you need to know your way around a seam and the terms used to describe the different parts.

PREPARATION

As with most things in dressmaking, the secret is in good preparation. You should pin and then baste (tack) all your seams until you become more confident. Once you have made a few garments, you can simply pin straight seams. Basting is a temporary hand-worked running stitch that holds your seam together accurately, ready for machining.

Common seam allowances used in dressmaking (and in the projects in this book):

- ⅝ in. (1.5 cm)
- ⅜ in. (1 cm) on some pocket edges
- ¾ in. (2 cm) where a lapped zip is used.

Each project tells you what seam allowance to use at the start of the instructions.

Seam line—the stitching line

Seam allowance—the distance between the stitched seam line and the edge of the fabric

Basting (tacking)

1 Place the pieces to be joined right sides together and the cut edges of the seam allowances level. Pin each end of the seam, match up any notches, and then pin in between to prevent the fabric from stretching.

2 Thread your needle with a single length of thread (doubled thread is more likely to tangle) in a contrasting color to that of your fabric. Don't make a knot in the end. The long end of the thread should be roughly the length of your forearm (very long threads will also be more likely to tangle).

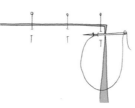

3 To start your line of basting, make a small stitch at the beginning of the seam. Make 2 more small stitches on top of the 1st. This is just as–if not more–secure than a knot.

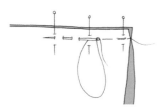

4 You can now work a line of small running stitches about ⅜ in. (1 cm) long and ⅜ in. (1 cm) apart along the seam line. Try and baste on the seam line.

5 Finish the line of the basting in the same way that you started, with three small stitches on top of each other. Take the pins out as you go or at the end.

MACHINING THE SEAM

1 Set up your machine to sew a medium-length straight stitch and set the tension appropriate for your fabric. Make sure you have removed all the pins. Don't start machining right on the very edge of the fabric, as there won't be enough fabric for your machine to get hold of; a good guide is to make sure the hole in the presser foot is covered by your fabric.

2 Bring the needle down into the fabric by turning the hand wheel toward you and then use your foot pedal. If you always start sewing in this way, your machine will never get in a tangle before you've even started.

3 Use the seam guides on your machine to make sure that your seam is accurate and straight. Do a reverse stitch to reinforce the start of the seam.

4 When you reach the end of your seam, don't sew off the fabric. Do a reverse stitch to reinforce the end of the seam, then take your foot off the foot pedal and bring up the needle to its highest position using the hand wheel again (remember to turn it toward you). You will always be able to easily remove your fabric from the machine if you stop in this position.

5 Once your seam is sewn you can remove basting stitches and press the seam open from the wrong side of the fabric.

NEATENING SEAM ALLOWANCES

In woven fabrics cut edges will fray, which is messy and will eventually weaken your seam. Here are some ways to neaten your seam allowances, along with what fabrics and types of seam they're best suited for.

Simple zig-zag Suitable for most fabrics and for both straight and curved seams, this is the easiest and quickest method, although not necessarily the neatest.

1 This method uses a zig-zag stitch sewn along the edges of the seam allowances. You get the best result if you have an overcasting or overlock foot for your sewing machine. If your machine didn't come with one, you should be able to buy one.

2 Set your machine up to sew a zig-zag stitch on the maximum width and a slightly shorter than medium stitch length (i.e. if your machine's stitch length goes up to 4, set it to 1.5). You will need to loosen your tension by one setting to make sure the zig-zag stitches don't pucker your fabric.

3 Start your zig-zag stitch in the same way as described in step 2 for machining your seam, but don't reverse stitch.

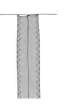

4 With an overcasting foot, the stitch will go right over the edge of the fabric; follow the instructions for your particular overcasting foot for exactly where to position your fabric.

5 You can still zig-zag seam allowances using a normal presser foot. Position the zig-zagging a bit further in from the cut edge of the fabric.

Bias binding Bias binding looks a bit like a strip of plain woven cotton fabric with each of the long edges folded in toward the wrong side of the fabric. It is cut on the bias (see Fabrics, page 132) so that it can stretch around curves.

Simple bound edge Suitable for most fabrics, although the binding may form a ridge along the outside of the garment in lighter weight fabrics. If it does, use the Hong Kong method instead. Great for straight and curved seams and fabrics that fray a lot, this method is time consuming but very neat.

1 Open out one side of the folded binding and place the right side of the binding on the wrong side of the seam allowance. Position the edge of the binding so that it just overhangs the cut edge of the fabric. Pin, baste (tack) if necessary, and machine in place along the crease line of the binding.

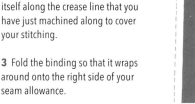

2 Let the binding fold back on itself along the crease line that you have just machined along to cover your stitching.

3 Fold the binding so that it wraps around onto the right side of your seam allowance.

4 The loose folded edge of the binding, now on the right side of the seam allowance, should be able to just cover your first line of stitching. Pin, baste if necessary, and machine it in place as close as you can to this loose folded edge.

Hong Kong finish
Slightly easier to do than the simple bound edge, this method is great for almost any seam in any fabric.

1 Unfold one of the long pre-folded edges of the bias binding and press to remove the crease.

2 Open out the edge of the binding that is still folded and place the right side of the binding on the right side of your seam allowance. Make sure the edge of the binding and the edge of the fabric are level. Pin, baste (tack) if necessary, and machine in place along the crease line.

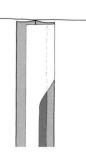

3 Let the binding fold back on itself along the crease line that you have just machined along to cover your stitching.

4 Fold along the center of the binding so that it folds around onto the wrong side of the seam allowance.

5 The loose, unfolded edge of the binding is now on the wrong side of the seam allowance and will easily cover your first line of stitching.

6 Pin it in place from the right side of the seam allowance. Baste if necessary and machine it in place from the right side of the seam allowance along the first seam you stitched.

Snipping seam allowances on curved seams

Curved seams need to have their seam allowances snipped so that the curve can lie flat and the seam will be nice and smooth. Machine the seam and neaten the seam allowances using one of the methods described on page 137.

1 For inside curves, use small sharp-pointed scissors to make a simple snip into the seam allowance at regular intervals along the seam, close to the seam line.

2 For outside curves, snip small triangles out of the seam allowance at regular intervals along the seam, close to the seam line.

UNDERSTITCHING

Understitching is done along the edges of a garment, usually edges with a facing, such as pocket openings in skirts. When a seam is understitched, the line of understitching magically pulls the seam line that would be on the edge of the garment (for example, around the waist of a skirt) toward the inside of the garment so that the seam can't roll to the outside, leaving the facing visible.

Understitching is always done immediately after a seam has been sewn and before you move on to the next stage of making your garment.

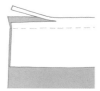

1 If your seam is curved, clip it (see Snipping seam allowances on curved seams, above). Then trim off approximately ¼ in. (5 mm) from the seam allowance of the facing only. This is known as "layering" and reduces the bulkiness of seams.

2 Gently press both seam allowances toward the facing from the wrong side of the garment.

3 Working from the right side so that you can easily see to keep your understitching a nice even distance from the original seam line, machine another line of stitching all along the seam about ⅛ in. (3 mm) from the original seam line. Keep checking on the underneath that the seam allowances are still lying toward the facing; don't let them roll back toward the garment.

TOPSTITCHING

Topstitching can be used to highlight certain seams, add decoration or contrast to a plain garment, hold bulky seam allowances flat, and keep edges crisp and flat (i.e. collars and cuffs or pocket openings). It is done from the right side of the fabric and is visible in the finished garment, so it needs to be neat!

It's best to use specialist topstitching thread on your machine, as regular thread can get lost on all but the lightest weight fabrics. You will also need a regular thread in a matching color for the bobbin.

Topstitching is easiest when done immediately after a seam has been sewn, so machine your seam, press it, and neaten the seam allowances first.

1 To topstitch either side of a seam, set your machine up to sew a regular straight stitch on a slightly longer than medium stitch length–i.e. if your stitch length goes up to 4, use stitch length 3.

2 The key to neat topstitching is to keep it a nice consistent distance from the seam line. An edgestitch foot is handy for this, as you can set the guide to follow your seam line. If you don't have an edgestitch foot, simply line up the seam line with something on your presser foot and try to keep it in the same position all the time you are sewing.

3 Machine the topstitching as you would do a seam, with a short reverse stitch at either end. Repeat along the other side of the seam line.

4 To topstitch along an edge do exactly the same, but line the edge up with something on your presser foot or use an edgestitch foot.

HEMS

A hem is a way of finishing the edges of a garment, most commonly along the lower edge. I'm going to show you four ways to sew a hem that are suitable for woven fabrics, along with some tips about which fabrics and hem types they are best suited for and how to keep your hems neat and accurate. Knitted fabrics need to be hemmed differently in order to keep their stretch; see Sewing Knitted Fabrics, page 134.

Hemming usually comes at the end of making a garment, often when you are impatient to get it finished so you can wear it. Don't rush it, though—a wonky hem will always be the first thing that catches the eye in an otherwise beautifully made garment!

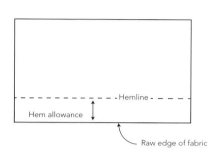

First, you need to know your way around a hem and the terms used to describe the different parts.

All the projects in this book use a ¾-in. (2-cm) hem allowance. As a general rule, the thicker the fabric the more of a hem allowance you need. You will often find up to 2-in. (5-cm) hem allowances on heavy coats, but as little as ³⁄₈ in. (1 cm) on lightweight silk garments.

To ensure your hems are neat and accurate, I recommend marking the hemline with a line of basting (tacking); mark it first with chalk on the wrong side of the fabric, then baste along the chalk line in a contrasting color of thread so that it is visible from the right side of the garment.

See Seams, page 136, for tips on zig-zag stitching and machine settings.

NEATENED AND TURNED HEM

The quickest hem (although not the neatest), this is suitable for all fabrics but tricky to do on a very curved hem–for example, the Hollings Circle Skirt (page 34).

1 First, zig-zag the raw edge of the hem allowance.

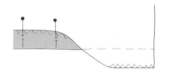

2 Fold the hem along the basted hemline to the wrong side of the garment and pin and baste in place along the middle of the zig-zag stitches. Give the hem a light press along the fold from the wrong side to get a crisp hemline.

> **TIP**
> Try to avoid pressing the basting (tacking) stitches, as basting can leave indentation marks behind on some fabrics when pressed.

3 Set your machine to sew a straight stitch and machine the hem from the right side of your garment, following the basting stitches. (Machine stitching usually looks best from the upper, or needle, side rather than the bobbin side, so this allows you to have that better stitching on the outside of your garment.)

4 Remove all the basting stitches and press the hem thoroughly from the wrong side to get a nice, crisp hem.

DOUBLE-TURNED HEM

Neater than the neatened and turned hem, but more bulky due to the fabric being turned twice and results in quite a narrow hem, a double-turned hem is best for lighter-weight fabrics because of the bulk.

1 Fold the raw edge of the hem allowance to the wrong side of the garment so that the cut edge is level with the basted hemline, and press.

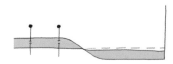

2 Fold the fabric to the wrong side again, along the basted hemline. Press and pin in place. Baste in place close to the first folded edge.

3 Set your machine to sew a straight stitch and machine the hem from the right side of your garment following the basting stitches. (Machine stitching usually looks best from the upper, or needle, side rather than the bobbin side, so this allows you to have that better stitching on the outside of your garment.)

4 Remove all the basting stitches and press the hem thoroughly from the wrong side to get a nice, crisp hem.

HAND BLIND HEM OR SLIPSTITCHED HEM

A blind hem is very neat, leaving no visible stitches on the outside of the garment when done well. More time consuming than other methods, it is suitable for all fabrics and hem types as it is easier to manipulate any excess fabric in curved hems when sewing by hand than by machine.

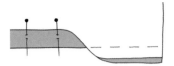

TIP
Keep your stitches along the hem allowance fold quite short and close together, as this isn't the strongest of hems.

1 Fold the raw edge of the hem allowance to the wrong side of the garment by just ¼ in. (5 mm) and press.

2 Fold the fabric to the wrong side again, along the basted hemline. Press and pin in place.

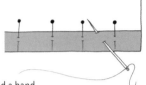

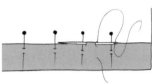

3 Thread a hand sewing needle with a thread color to match your fabric. Feed the needle into the turned-up hem allowance only (not going through to the right side of the garment) and bring the needle out along the upper folded edge of the turned-up hem allowance.

4 Make a few tiny stitches in the hem allowance to secure the start of your sewing.

5 Make a tiny stitch in the garment, above the fold in the hem allowance, catching just a few threads of the fabric.

6 Directly opposite on the hem, slide the needle along the folded edge of the pinned-up hem.

7 Repeat steps 5 and 6 all around the hem.

BIAS-FACED HEM

Probably my favorite method for hemming as it gives a really neat finish, I use it a lot on my garments. It's suitable for most fabrics except very thin lightweight ones and is the ideal method for dealing with tricky curved hems like the circle skirt (page 34).

1 This method requires only a ⅝-in. (1.5-cm) hem allowance. Either cut away the excess ¼ in. (5 mm) or, if you're happy for your finished skirt to be a tiny bit longer, leave it as it is.

2 Fold the short end of the binding to the wrong side by about ¾ in. (2 cm). Press to keep it in place.

3 Open out one long edge of the folded binding and place the right side of the folded-back short end on the right side of the hem. Position the opened-out edge of the binding level with the raw edge of the hem allowance. Pin in place and baste if necessary.

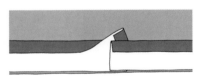

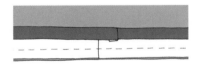

4 When you get back to where you started, allow the other short end of the binding to overlap the start by approx. ¾ in. (2 cm).

5 With your machine set to a regular straight stitch, machine along the crease line in the binding.

6 Fold the binding back on itself on the crease line that you have just machined along to cover your stitching.

7 Fold the fabric along the marked hemline, so that *all* the binding folds around to the inside of the hem. Pin the loose folded edge of the binding, which is now on the wrong side of the hem on the inside of your garment, in place and baste close to the upper edge of the binding. Avoiding the basting stitches, give the hem a light press along the fold and the binding from the wrong side to get a crisp hemline that will be easier to machine.

8 With a regular straight stitch, machine the hem in place from the right side following the basting stitches.

9 Remove the basting stitches and press the hem to get a crisp edge.

USING ELASTIC

In this book, I have used elastic for two different waistband finishes (one uses a casing and the other applies the elastic directly to the garment) and to add gathers to a garment. Whatever you plan to use your elastic for, make sure you choose good-quality elastic which should easily stretch to approximately twice its length and recover (snap back to its original size) quickly.

ELASTICATED WAISTBANDS

When choosing elastic for waistbands, the wider the better. Narrow elastic tends to dig into your body and can easily twist when inserted into a separate waistband, I recommend using elastic at least 1¼ in. (3 cm) wide for maximum comfort.

Method 1: Using a separate waistband
This method involves feeding elastic through a separate waistband applied to your garment and is used in the Roewood Jersey Pencil Skirt.

1 Following the project instructions, make and attach the waistband.

2 Cut your elastic long enough to fit your waist comfortably and allow an extra 1¼ in. (3 cm) to join the ends.

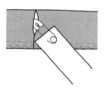

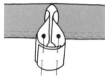

3 Once you have cut the elastic to length, attach one end to a safety pin and start to feed it through the gap left in the waistband.

4 When you reach the beginning again, pull both ends of the elastic fully out of the waistband, overlap the ends by 1¼ in. (3 cm), and pin them together.

5 Using a regular straight stitch on your sewing machine, carefully sew the ends together. I tend to sew a square with a cross in the middle.

6 Let the elastic pull back into the waistband and close the gap in the waistband using a hand slipstitch. (See Attaching Waistbands–Attaching a Plain Waistband, step 14, page 148.)

Method 2: Exposed elastic waistband
This method involves stitching your elastic directly onto the waist of your garment and is used in the elasticated waist version of the Hollings Circle Skirt.

1 Neaten the waist edge of the skirt with a zig-zag stitch (see Seams–Neatening Seam Allowances, page 137).

2 Cut your elastic long enough to fit your waist comfortably and allow an extra 1¼ in. (3 cm) to join the ends.

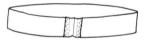

3 Once you have cut the elastic to length, join the short ends with a regular seam, to form a circle. Neaten the two cut edges of the elastic with a zig-zag stitch (see Seams–Neatening Seam Allowances, page 137).

4 With the seam open, topstitch the seam allowances down onto the elastic.

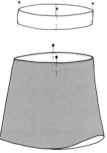

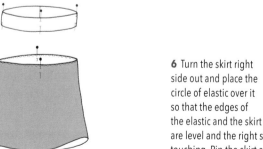

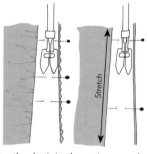

5 Mark the center front and center back of the skirt with pins. Divide the circle of elastic into four and mark three of the four points with pins (the fourth is marked by the seam joining the two ends of the elastic together).

6 Turn the skirt right side out and place the circle of elastic over it so that the edges of the elastic and the skirt are level and the right sides of the fabric and elastic are touching. Pin the skirt and elastic together at the four marked points.

7 In between the pinned points, stretch the elastic to fit the skirt and pin again.

8 Machine the elastic in place using a regular straight stitch: use a narrow seam allowance (use the edge of your presser foot as a guide and keep the edges of the skirt and elastic level with it), sew a few stitches to start and reverse to secure the stitching, then with one hand in front of the presser foot and one hand behind, stretch the elastic to fit the skirt in between the pinned sections and machine. Even though you're holding the fabric and elastic tight and stretched, you must still allow the machine to feed the fabric through, don't hold it so tight that it doesn't go anywhere! When you get to a pin, remove it and continue to the next one holding the elastic stretched. Do another reverse stitch when you get back to the start of your seam to secure the stitching.

USING ELASTIC TO ADD GATHERS

Elastic can be directly stitched into strategic parts of garments to add gathers. Elastic used for this task is quite narrow, as it is usually attached to a seam allowance. I recommend using elastic approximately ⅜ in. (1 cm) wide; this is narrow enough to fit on a seam allowance and wide enough to be easy to sew. This technique is used to add the gathers in the gathered side seams version of the Roewood Jersey Pencil Skirt.

1 Cut your elastic to the length given in the "You Will Need" list for the size that you are making.

2 Cut the elastic in half.

3 Pin one end of one piece of elastic to the dot marked on the side seam, so that the end of the elastic extends ⅜ in. (1 cm) beyond the dot.

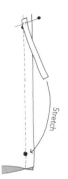

4 Pin the other end of the elastic to the lower placement dot on the same side seam, so that the elastic extends ⅜ in. (1 cm) beyond the dot.

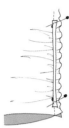

5 Machine a few straight stitches to secure the elastic to the first dot; you should be stitching the elastic directly on top of your seamline, not on the seam allowance. Reverse stitch to secure.

6 With one hand in front of the presser foot and one hand behind, stretch the elastic to fit the side seam of the skirt in between the pinned dots, and machine. Do another reverse stitch when you get to the second dot to secure the stitching. Trim off the overhanging ends of the elastic.

DARTS

Darts give three-dimensional shape to a flat piece of fabric. They are used to fit garments around curved parts of the body; in skirts, this is the waist and hips.

Edge of pattern piece

The point of a dart always aims toward the area of fullness on the body that it is shaping the fabric around–for example; a waist dart in a skirt points toward the hips.

1 Mark the point and the two wide ends of the dart on the wrong side of your fabric with tailor's chalk or a marking pencil (see Transferring Pattern Markings, page 133), then connect the marks to draw in the sides of the dart, using a ruler to get a straight line. Now you have a stitching line to follow.

2 With right sides together, fold along the center of the dart to the point, so that the two stitching lines lie on top of each other. Pin and baste (tack) in place along the marked stitching line.

3 Start machining at the wide end of the dart, on the edge of the fabric. Do a reverse stitch to secure your stitching.

4 At the point of the dart, gradually trail your stitching off the fabric so that the last stitch lands just off the edge of the fabric. Don't reverse stitch at the point of your dart. Knot the threads securely and cut the ends to approx. ⅜ in. (1 cm) long.

5 This will make the point of your dart nice and flat. If you reverse stitch or finish sewing too far from the fold of the fabric at the point of the dart, you will get a little pouch rather than a smooth point at the end.

6 Press the dart toward the center front or center back of your garment over a tailor's ham (see Tools & Equipment, page 129). Using a ham allows you to press the whole length of the dart and maintain the 3-D shape that it's started to form rather than flattening it. If you don't have a ham, use the end of your ironing board when pressing your dart to maintain its shape.

ZIPPERS

Zippers can often strike fear in the heart of those new to sewing. Don't let them; the secret to a well-inserted zipper is all in the preparation. The more care you take preparing, the easier your zipper will be to sew and the better the results. I'm going to show you three different zippers, each of them suited to different types of fabrics and garments.

Zippers come in standard lengths. The length of a zipper refers to the length of the teeth—the fastening part of the zipper, from the stopper at the top to the plastic or metal stopper at the bottom. The zipper tapes extend beyond the stoppers at each end and aren't included in the stated zipper length. For the projects in this book you will be using closed-end plastic or metal zippers and invisible or concealed zippers only.

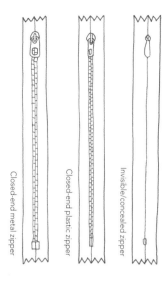

Closed-end metal zipper

Closed-end plastic zipper

Invisible/concealed zipper

CENTERED OR SLOT ZIPPER

A centered or slot zipper is the easiest way to insert a zipper into a garment and is most often used in the center back seam. It has stitching visible on the outside of the garment and forms two flaps of fabric that cover the zipper with an opening down the center. It works well for a wide range of fabric types and weights, although it can be difficult to insert well on very thick fabric such as heavyweight denim or heavy wools.

It can be used in the following projects: Fallowfield Pencil Skirt, Hollings Circle Skirt, Rusholme A-Line Skirt.

1 Neaten the raw edges of the seam allowances of the seam where the zipper will go. Baste (tack) the full length of the seam accurately and securely on the seam line. (See Seams, page 136.) I sometimes find machine basting can give better results for this. To machine baste, set up your machine to sew a straight stitch, set the stitch length to maximum, and set the tension 1 setting lower than required for your fabric.

2 Machine the seam with a regular straight stitch from the hem to the base of the zipper position (marked with a dot on your pattern). Don't take out the basting stitches. Press the seam open along its full length.

3 Place the zipper face down on the pressed-open seam, on the wrong side of the garment, positioning the metal stopper on the bottom of the zipper just above the end of your machine sewing. The teeth of the zipper should be centered on the pressed-open seam.

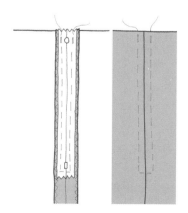

4 Starting at the base of the zipper, pin each side of the zipper onto the seam, ensuring that the teeth stay centered over the seam. Pin all the way through the zipper tape, the seam allowances, and the skirt, so that the pins show on the right side of the skirt.

6 Make sure your basting goes all the way through to the right side of the skirt—you're not just basting the zipper to the seam allowances. This basting will act as a guide for your machine sewing. Take out the top 1¼ in. (3 cm) of basting you did in step 1 that holds the seam covering the zipper closed. This will allow you to move the zipper pull out of the way when you're machine sewing.

5 Baste the zipper in place, keeping your stitches quite small and as straight as you can down the center of each side of the zipper. Start at the waist edge of one side of the zipper, work your way along the center of the zipper tape, take a few stitches across the bottom of the zipper (under the stopper), and continue up the other side.

7 Put a zipper foot on your sewing machine. Open the zipper a little way and start sewing on a regular straight stitch down one side of the zipper from the top waist edge, reverse stitching at the beginning of your stitching. When you reach the zipper pull, stop with the needle down, lift the presser foot, slide the zipper pull up out of the way, lower the presser foot again, and continue sewing.

8 Following your basting stitches, sew to approx. ⅝ in. (1.5 cm) above the end of the basting. Then, with the needle down, lift the presser foot and turn the fabric to sew the last part at an angle (forming a V when done on both sides). Don't reverse stitch: try and get your last stitch to land in the seam. Pull the threads through to the wrong side and knot them.

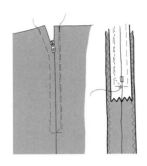

9 Repeat with the other side, remembering to open the zipper to start. You should end up with a V at the base of your zipper.

LAPPED ZIPPER

Most often used for side-seam zippers, this method also has stitching visible on the outside of the garment and forms one large flap of fabric that fully covers the zipper, with an opening down one side. It works well on a wide range of fabrics, but is best avoided in very heavy or thick fabric. This type of zipper is easier to sew if you have a slightly larger seam allowance to work with. As it is only used in the Roehampton Culottes project, I have increased the seam allowance on the side seams of this project to ¾ in. (2 cm).

1 Neaten the raw edges of the seam allowances of the seam where the zipper will go. Baste (tack) the full length of the seam accurately and securely on the seam line. (See Seams, page 136.) As with the centered zipper, I sometimes find machine basting can give better results.

2 Machine the seam with a regular straight stitch from the hem to the base of the zipper position (marked with a dot on your pattern). Don't take out the basting stitches. Press the seam open along its full length.

3 Place the zipper face down on the pressed-open seam on the wrong side of the garment, positioning the metal stopper on the bottom of the zipper just above the end of your machine sewing. The teeth of the zipper will now not be centered over the seam.) Pin the zipper to the seam allowance of the back skirt only (not all the way through the garment). This will be the underlap.

4 Put a zipper foot on your sewing machine and stitch the pinned zipper tape to the seam allowance only. Stitch close to the zipper teeth.

5 Fold the zipper over away from the seam allowance, so that you're looking at the right side of the zipper (the seam allowance will cover the line of stitching you've just done) and stitch again close to the fold.

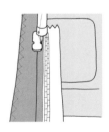

6 When you get close to the zipper pull, stop with the needle down, lift up the presser foot, and slide the zipper pull out of the way. Put the foot down again and continue to the end of the zipper tape.

7 Close the zipper and lay the skirt out flat, looking at the wrong side. Pull the loose side of the zipper over onto the other seam allowance and place it just inside the edge of the seam allowance, level with the zig-zagging. Pin and baste the unattached side of the zipper onto the other seam allowance (this should be the seam allowance of the front skirt), but this time going through all the layers. This side will be the overlap and this basting will be visible on the outside of your garment and will act as a guide for your machine stitching.

8 Remove the original basting that was holding the seam together over the zipper a little way, so that you can open the zipper. With your zipper foot still on the machine, stitch on a regular straight stitch, following the basting done in step 7. At the bottom of the zipper, stitch across at right angles and stop when you reach the seam line. Reverse stitch at the start of this line of stitching at the waist edge, but don't reverse at the end when you reach the seam line. Pull the threads through to the wrong side and knot them.

INVISIBLE OR CONCEALED ZIPPER

A really neat zipper style with no stitching visible from the outside of the garment, it should almost look as if the seam of the garment is magically separating when the zipper is opened.

An invisible zipper can be used in the following projects: Fallowfield Pencil Skirt, Finsbury Bubble Skirt, Hollings Circle Skirt, Roehampton Culottes, Rusholme A-Line Skirt. Before you start:

• Buy a zipper longer than you need (the zipper lengths stated in the project "You Will Need" lists include this extra length).

• Apply strips of iron-on interfacing to the wrong sides of the seam allowances of delicate fabrics to avoid stretching the fabric and to support the zipper.

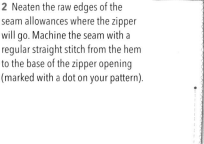

1 With the zipper open to help the teeth unroll, carefully press the wrong side of each zipper tape with a COOL iron.

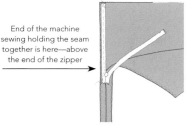

End of the machine sewing holding the seam together is here—above the end of the zipper

2 Neaten the raw edges of the seam allowances where the zipper will go. Machine the seam with a regular straight stitch from the hem to the base of the zipper opening (marked with a dot on your pattern).

3 Open the zipper. Place one side of the zipper with the right side of one of the seam allowances. The zipper teeth should be level with the seam line, and the edge of the zipper tape and the zig-zagged edge of the seam allowance should be on the same side. The zipper will extend beyond the end of your machining i.e. beyond the dot for the end of your zipper..

4 Pin the zipper in place and hand baste (tack) with small secure stitches until you reach the end of the machined seam and the dot marking the end of the zipper. At this point, taper your basting out toward the edge of the seam allowance and zipper tape. This makes it easier to open and close the zipper later.

5 Close the zipper and pin the other side of the zipper to the other seam allowance, making sure that the tops of the zipper and the tops of the seam remain level. Lay the skirt out with the right sides of the fabric touching to check this and to start your pinning. Make sure the zipper teeth are positioned accurately along the seam line again.

6 Keep the zipper closed this time and hand baste in place again, tapering the basting out when you reach the end of the machined seam.

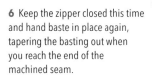

7 Open the zipper fully; you will need to feed the zipper pull right down to the end of the zipper tapes, as the seam is stitched higher than the end of the zipper so there's only a small gap to feed it through. This is why your basting tapers out toward the edge of the seam allowance.

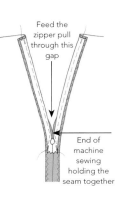

Feed the zipper pull through this gap

End of machine sewing holding the seam together

8 Put an invisible zipper foot on your sewing machine. The right foot for your make and model machine will be better than a universal one.

9 Lay your skirt out with the two panels of fabric on top of each other, right sides together, with the zipper on the left-hand side. Lift the top layer of fabric back so that you can feed the teeth of the zipper on the under layer of fabric into the right-hand groove in the invisible zipper foot.

10 Using a regular straight stitch, sew the zipper in place. Don't reverse at the start and end of this stitching; instead, pull the threads through to the wrong side of the seam allowance once you have finished machining and knot them. While machining, keep your fingers close to the front of the invisible zipper foot and help the zipper teeth unroll so they feed through the foot more easily.

11 Machine until you reach the end of the stitching holding the seam together. This row of machining and the machining holding the seam together should be level.

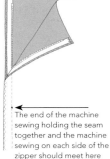

The end of the machine sewing holding the seam together and the machine sewing on each side of the zipper should meet here

12 Repeat with the other side of the zipper and the other groove in the zipper foot.

13 Once you have secured the ends of your machining, remove the basting and feed the zipper pull through the gap between the end of the machining holding the seam together and the open zipper.

ATTACHING WAIST FACINGS

A waist facing can be used as an alternative to a waistband to finish the waist of a skirt. Unlike a waistband, a facing isn't visible from the outside of the skirt as it is formed from a layer of fabric attached to the waist edge and then folded over to the inside.

Waist facings don't work well on skirt styles that are very full with a lot of fabric to be supported, as in a gathered waist (like the Finsbury Bubble Skirt and Brighton Front-opening Skirt), a waist with pleats (like the pleated versions of the Rusholme A-line Skirt and Roehampton Culottes), or in skirt styles with front cut-away pockets (like the pocket versions of the Rusholme A-line Skirt and Roehampton Culottes).

The Fallowfield Pencil Skirt, Rusholme A-line Skirt, and Granville Wrap Skirt all have the option to finish the waist with a facing. The Granville Wrap Skirt has its own facing pattern pieces, while the Fallowfield Pencil Skirt and the Rusholme A-line Skirt use the same waist-facing pattern pieces.

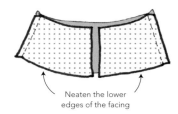

Neaten the lower edges of the facing

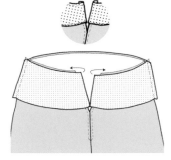

1 As directed in the project instructions, apply interfacing to the facing pieces, and re-mark any pattern markings covered by the interfacing. Join the side seams of the front and back facings. Press the seams open and neaten the raw edges of the seam allowances (see Neatening Seam Allowances, page 137).

2 Neaten the lower edge of the front and back facing strip with either a zig-zag stitch or by attaching bias binding (see Bias Binding, page 137).

3 With the zipper open and the skirt right side out, place the waist facing on the waist edge of the skirt, right sides together. Match the side seams first and pin in place, making sure ⅝ in. (1.5 cm) extends beyond the zipper at each end of the facing. Wrap the extending ends of the facing back around to the wrong side of the skirt to cover the zipper. Pin the whole length of the facing in place and baste (tack) securely.

TIP

By machining with the skirt layer on top, you can make sure that the seams remain pressed open and the darts stay pressed in the right direction.

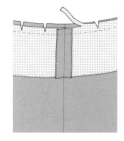

4 With the skirt layer on top, taking a ⅝ in. (1.5-cm) seam allowance, machine the waist facings in place.

5 Clip the curved seam allowances; if your fabric is thick and bulky (heavy denim or thicker), trim back the seam allowance of the facing only to half its current width. This is called "layering" and helps to stop the seam from becoming too bulky.

6 Press the seam allowances toward the facing and understitch the waist seam (see Understitching, page 138).

7 Turn the facing to the inside of the skirt and finish the short loose ends of the facing around the zipper by hand, using an invisible slipstitch. Pin the facing in place, with the folded edge of the facing sitting away from the zipper teeth. Thread a hand sewing needle with matching thread—a single thread without a knot. Insert the needle into the facing and bring it out at one end of the folded edge.

8 Make a few tiny stitches on the fold to secure the start of your sewing, then make a tiny stitch on the zipper tape, taking care not to go through to the right side of the skirt.

9 Directly opposite on the facing, slide the needle along the folded edge.

10 Repeat to the end of the edge of the facing. Finish in the same way you started, with a few small stitches. The thread ends can be cut close to the fabric. Do the same with the other side of the zipper and facing.

ADDING HANGING LOOPS

1 Follow steps 1 and 2 of attaching a waist facing.

2 Cut two pieces of narrow (¼ in./5 mm) cotton tape, each 12 in. (30 cm) long.

3 Fold one length of tape in half and pin it onto the right side of the waist of the skirt, positioning the tape in line with the side seam of the skirt, with the ends of the tape level with the raw edge.

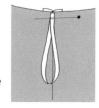

4 Machine the loop in place with a line of straight stitch just ⅜ in. (1 cm) long; any longer and the loop will be attached to the outside of the skirt beyond the facing seam. Repeat with the other tape loop and the other side seam.

5 Continue attaching the waist facing from step 3. Your hanging loops will now be secured in the waist seam. Be careful not to catch the loops when doing your understitching by making sure they lie away from the facing, toward the skirt.

ADDITIONAL FASTENINGS

A well-fitted zipper that reaches the waist seam should eliminate the need for any additional fastenings at the top of the facing, but if you feel you need something extra, attach a hook and eye (see Buttons & Other Fastenings, page 150).

ATTACHING WAISTBANDS

A separate waistband adds strength to the waist of a skirt and ensures that the waist keeps its shape and doesn't stretch out of shape. All the skirts in this book are designed to sit on the natural waist, meaning we can use the simplest form of waistband: a one-piece straight waistband.

The waistband patterns for the projects vary in width from 1 to 1⅜ in. (2.5 to 3.5 cm). If you want to you can change this width, but I recommend going no narrower than 1 in. (2.5 cm) and no wider than 2 in. (5 cm) to ensure that the waistband still fits flat against the body without gaping.

The Fallowfield Pencil Skirt, Finsbury Bubble Skirt, and Rusholme A-line Skirt all use the same waistband pattern. Instructions are included to draft your own waistband for the Hollings Circle Skirt.

All waistbands have the center front and center back positions marked with notches and the side-seam positions marked with dots.

ATTACHING A PLAIN WAISTBAND

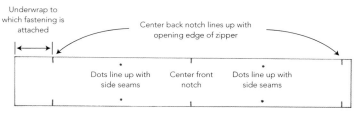

Underwrap to which fastening is attached

Center back notch lines up with opening edge of zipper

Dots line up with side seams

Center front notch

Dots line up with side seams

1 Once you have applied the interfacing to your waistband, make sure all the pattern markings are still visible on both of the long edges.

2 At each end of the waistband along the long edges, there are notches to line up with the opening where your zipper is located; this will be at either the center back or the side seam, depending on the skirt you're making. At one end the notch is positioned the width of the seam allowance in from the short end of the waistband. At the other end, the notch is positioned 2⅛ in. (5.5 cm) in from the short end of the waistband;

this end forms an "underwrap" onto which you can attach a fastening once the waistband is attached. On skirts with a center back zipper, it doesn't matter which side of the back skirt this underwrap is positioned on, but on the Roehampton Culottes (page 92), which have a side zipper, this underwrap needs to be positioned on the back side seam.

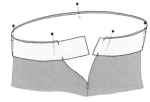

3 With right sides together, making sure these notches line up with the opening edge of the zipper, pin one long edge of the waistband to the skirt. Depending on where your skirt opens, line up the center front and center back notches on the waistband with the center front and center back of the skirt and pin in place, then line up the dots on the waistband with the side seams in the skirt and pin in place.

4 Once all your markings and seams are aligned and pinned in place, pin the gaps in between.

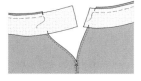

5 Baste (tack) the waistband in place, then remove the pins. Machine on a regular straight stitch with the skirt layer on top so that you can make sure pressed-open seams and pressed darts remain in the right positions. Ensure that your seam allowance is accurate so that the waistband seam is level at each side of the zipper once it is closed.

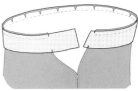

6 On curved waist edges (Hollings Circle Skirt, Rusholme A-line Skirt, and Roehampton Culottes), snip into the seam allowance of the skirt layer only (not the waistband) close to the machine stitching so that the curve can sit flat.

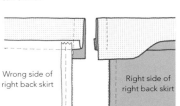

Wrong side of right back skirt

Right side of right back skirt

9 Fold the waistband along the length, right sides together. At the end without the underwrap (the end that only has a seam allowance extending beyond the zipper), pin the short ends of the waistband together and unfold the seam allowance of the long loose edge that you pressed in the last step. Baste and machine level with the zipper teeth from the folded top edge of the waistband, stopping at the crease where you have unfolded the pressed seam allowance on the long loose edge of the waistband. This is easiest to machine with the loose edge of the waistband on top.

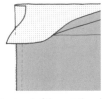

11 At each short end of the waistband, press both seam allowances at the corner over the seam onto the waistband. This helps to form a sharp corner when the waistband is turned through to the right side.

7 Remove the basting stitches and press the seam up toward the waistband.

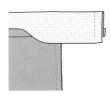

10 (a) For narrow waistbands (less than 1⅜ in./3.5 cm) and thicker fabrics like denim
Join the other end of the waistband (with the longer extension forming the underwrap) in the same way as described in step 9, machining the seam with a ⅝-in. (1.5-cm) seam allowance.

12 Turn the short ends of the waistband through to the right side. Use a thick knitting needle or a chopstick to poke out the corners until they are nice and sharp. Don't use scissors for this or you'll end up with a hole!

8 With the skirt wrong side out, press under the seam allowance along the other (loose) long edge of the waistband to the wrong side.

Right side of left back skirt

Wrong side of left back skirt

10 (b) For wider waistbands (over 1⅜ in./3.5 cm) in lighter-weight fabrics than denim
Fold the waistband along the length with the right sides together and unfold the pressed-up seam allowance on the long, loose edge of the waistband. Also unfold the pressed-up seam allowance on the attached edge so that the seam allowance lies toward the skirt. With the side of the waistband that is attached to the skirt on top (which now has the seam allowance folded down toward the skirt), pin and baste in place. Starting at the short end, machine in place, turn at the corner and follow the seam line until your basting meets the end of the machine stitching holding the waistband onto the skirt.

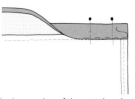

13 Bring the loose edge of the waistband with the pressed-under seam allowance down to the inside of the skirt, so that the folded edge is level with the first line of machining attaching the waistband to the skirt. Pin in place and baste close to the loose, folded edge of the waistband.

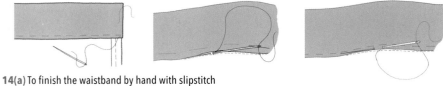

14(a) To finish the waistband by hand with slipstitch
Thread a hand sewing needle with matching thread—a single thread without a knot. Insert the needle into the waistband and bring it out along the folded edge of the waistband (left). Make a few tiny stitches on the fold to secure the start of your sewing. Make a tiny stitch on the skirt, along the previous line of machine stitching

(center). Directly opposite on the waistband, slide the needle along the folded edge (right). Repeat all the way around the waistband.Finish in the same way you started, with a few small stitches. The thread ends can be cut close to the fabric.

14(b) To finish the waistband by machine
Topstitching gives a quicker, stronger finish. Your basting (done in step 13) should go all the way through to the outside of the skirt and will be a guide for your machining, so keep it as neat as you can and an even distance from that folded edge. Machine in place from the right side of the skirt; if you position your machining just above your basting you will be sure to catch the underside of the waistband in your machining.

ATTACHING A WAISTBAND WITH A BIAS-BOUND FINISH

1 Follow steps 1–7 for Attaching a Plain Waistband (page 147).

2 Cut a length of bias binding to fit the waistband starting ¾ in. (2 cm) in from the seam line at each end.

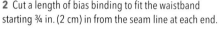

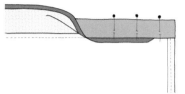

5 Bring the loose edge of the waistband with the bias binding down to the inside of the skirt, so that the seam in the binding is level with the first line of machining attaching the waistband to the skirt. At the ends of the waistband turn in the seam allowance; the end of the bias binding should taper into the seam. Pin in place.

3 To attach the binding use the instructions for Neatening Seam Allowances–Bias Binding on page 137, but, taper the ends of the binding off the fabric.

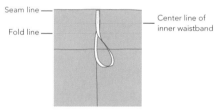

6 This method is best finished by machine rather than slipstitched by hand. Baste (tack) the loose edge of the waistband to the skirt just above the bias binding. The basting should go all the way through to the outside of the skirt and will be a guide for your machining, so keep it as neat as you can along the bias binding edge.

4 Continue as for plain waistbands steps 9–12, but ignore the references to the pressed seam allowance along this loose edge.

7 Machine in place from the right side of the skirt, if you position your machining just above your basting, you will be sure to catch the underside of the waistband in your machining.

ADDING HANGING LOOPS

1 Cut two pieces of narrow (¼ in./5 mm) cotton tape, each 12 in. (30 cm) long.

2 Follow steps 1–7 of Attaching a Plain Waistband.

3 Fold one length of tape in half and place it onto the right side of the waistband, positioning the tape in line with the side seam of the skirt, the ends of the tape level with the raw edge.

Seam line — | Fold line —

Center line of inner waistband

4 Mark the center line of the inner waistband and pin the loop in place from here to the raw edge of the waistband. Machine the loop in place with a line of straight stitch, stopping at the middle of the inner waistband. Repeat with the other tape loop and the other side seam.

5 Fold under the seam allowance along the edge of the waistband, allowing the ends of the tape loops to also fold under.

6 Continue attaching the waistband from step 9 of Attaching a Plain Waistband (page 147), making sure you don't catch the loops in any of the stitching.

POSITIONING FASTENINGS

1 You can use a button and buttonhole, hook and bar, or press stud to fasten the waistband. See Buttons & Other Fastenings, page 150, for how to attach them.

2 On the outside of the skirt on the underwrap (the end of the waistband that extends beyond the zipper), mark with chalk or a line of basting (tacking) a vertical line that is level with the zipper and a horizontal intersecting line to mark the center of the waistband. This will be the position for the center of the button if using a button and buttonhole, the outer edge of the bar if using a hook and bar, or the center of the socket if using a press stud.

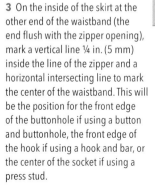

3 On the inside of the skirt at the other end of the waistband (the end flush with the zipper opening), mark a vertical line ¼ in. (5 mm) inside the line of the zipper and a horizontal intersecting line to mark the center of the waistband. This will be the position for the front edge of the buttonhole if using a button and buttonhole, the front edge of the hook if using a hook and bar, or the center of the socket if using a press stud.

BUTTONS & OTHER FASTENINGS

All of the skirts with waistbands in this book need some kind of fastening to secure the waistband at the top of the zipper. Hooks and bars are the neatest and most secure type of fastener for this job. The Brighton Front-opening Skirt has the option to have buttons, sew-on snaps, or no-sew snaps down the entire front of the skirt and so is a perfect project for practicing fastenings.

The positioning of your fastenings on waistbands is covered in Attaching Waistbands, page 147, including how to mark the positions. The marking of rows of fastenings as in the Brighton Front-opening Skirt is explained in that project's instructions.

BUTTONS AND BUTTONHOLES

Sewing a buttonhole on your sewing machine

1 Work out whether your machine does one-step or manual buttonholes. One-step machines will sew the whole buttonhole automatically and work out the correct length. Manual machines in some ways are more flexible, as you're not restricted in size by the button holder in the buttonhole foot, but you do have to work out the length of your buttonhole and mark it accurately on your fabric.

2 To work out the length that a buttonhole should be, measure the diameter of your button, then add ⅛ in./3 mm (¼ in./5 mm for thick fabrics such as heavyweight denim or thick wool).

Buttonhole length = button diameter plus ⅛ in./3mm or ¼ in./5 mm, depending on fabric thickness

3 Positioning
Rows of vertical buttonholes that fasten things like shirts and the front of the Brighton skirt should be placed directly on the center front line. Horizontal buttonholes should have their front edge placed ⅛ in. (3 mm) beyond the center front line to allow for a bit of give and movement and so as not to place the buttonhole under too much strain.

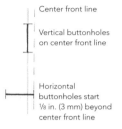

Center front line

Vertical buttonholes on center front line

Horizontal buttonholes start ⅛ in. (3 mm) beyond center front line

4 Marking
As buttonholes are sewn from the right side of the fabric, buttonholes need to be marked in a way that will be visible on the right side. The most accurate method is to transfer the markings from the paper pattern onto the wrong side of the fabric with a sharp piece of chalk, then stitch along the chalked lines with long basting (tacking) stitches in a contrasting color of thread to your fabric.

5 Once you have marked your buttonhole positions, place the front end of the marking in the center of the opening in the buttonhole foot. The cross made by your markings should be right in the center of the hole. Most machines sew buttonholes clockwise, starting at 6 o'clock.

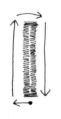

6 Sometimes machine-sewn buttonholes can look a bit sparsely stitched, leading to raggedy buttonholes once the fabric is cut. To reinforce the stitching, sew the buttonhole twice; don't remove the fabric in between, or the positioning of the second round of stitching will be wrong.

7 To cut the buttonhole open, place a pin across the bar tacks at the ends of the buttonhole to prevent cutting through them. Start in the center and pierce the fabric with an unpicker. Slide it to one end, turn, and slide it to the other. Alternatively use a pair of specialist buttonhole cutting scissors. Trim loose threads with sharp-pointed scissors.

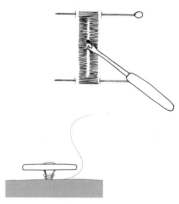

Sewing on a button by hand

1 When you sew on a button, place a toothpick over the top of the button and sew over it, as though you're sewing the toothpick to the button.

2 Once you have finished sewing the button, slide the toothpick out, pull the button to the end of the stitching, wrap your thread around the gap that's been formed between the button and the fabric, then feed the thread through to the wrong side of the fabric and fasten it off. (Skilled dressmakers will work buttonhole stitches or blanket stitches over the thread shank instead of simply wrapping the thread. This is a beautiful finishing touch to add to a garment, but something to aim for, rather than a necessity!)

3 This creates a thread shank so that the button can stand away from your garment and not sink into the fabric, meaning that your buttonhole will slide easily over your button and won't be under unnecessary strain that will weaken it.

HOOKS AND BARS

Attach the hook part to the inside of the overlap of the waistband (which sits on top when the skirt is worn) and the bar to the outside of the underwrap. The exact positioning is explained in detail in Attaching Waistbands, page 149. To attach them, simply sew through each hole in the hook and bar several times with small, evenly sized stitches. The stitching on the bar can go through all the layers; the stitching on the hook should go through the inner layer of the waistband only, as you don't want to see any stitching on the outside of the waistband. Make sure you finish off the ends of your threads securely.

SEW-ON SNAPS

Always choose a metal sew-on snap at least ³⁄₈ in. (1 cm) in diameter for maximum strength.

Attach the ball part to the inside of the overlap of the waistband (which sits on top when the skirt is worn) and the socket to the outside of the underwrap. To attach them, simply sew through each hole in the snap several times with small, evenly sized stitches. The stitching on the socket side (positioned on the underwrap) can go through all the layers; the stitching on the ball side should go through the inner layer of the waistband only, as you don't want to see any stitching on the outside of the waistband. Make sure you finish off the ends of your threads securely.

NO-SEW SNAPS

I have used no-sew snaps on the denim version of the Brighton Front-opening Skirt. They give a clean, modern finish and, as the name suggests, don't require any sewing.

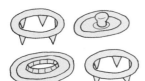

1 Each snap is formed of four parts: a ball side and a socket side, like the sew-on snaps, each on a post that goes through a hole pierced in the fabric. Each of these also has a spiked cover, which is positioned on the other side of the fabric and attaches to the ball or socket via the spikes that pierce through the fabric.

2 To attach them, you need a special gadget that is usually supplied with standard packs and can be used simply with a hammer. Follow the detailed instructions supplied with the pack.

3 You can buy a more sturdy, tripod-shaped applicator separately from the standard packs, which I have found gives much better, more consistent results. Follow the simple instructions supplied with the applicator.

GATHERING

Gathers are a way of putting fullness into a garment. Gathering can be done by hand, but I prefer to do it by machine as it is quicker and tends to be more even and easier to control.

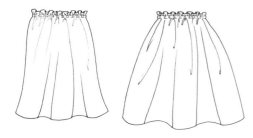

Gathering can look completely different depending on the type of fabric you are using; a lightweight, soft drapey fabric (far left) won't gain lots of fullness even with lots of gathers, but a crisper, heavier-weight fabric (left) will start to look quite balloon like and structured with the same amount of gathers.

GATHERING BY MACHINE

1 First neaten the edge that you are going to gather (see Seams, page 137).

2 Set up your sewing machine for a gathering stitch:
- Straight stitch
- Longest stitch length
- Loose needle tension (1 or 2 on a tension dial that goes up to 9)

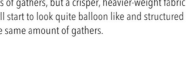

Positions for two rows of gathering

Seam line

3 You don't want your gathering stitches to be visible once the seam that the gathers will be secured into is stitched, so all gathering must be positioned inside the seam allowance. Start your first line of gathering just inside the seam line; for example, if your seam allowance is ⁵⁄₈ in. (1.5 cm), your first row of gathering stitches should be approx. ½ in. (1.3 cm) in from the edge.

4 Don't reverse stitch at the beginning of your machining; simply start sewing where instructed to in the project instructions. At the end of your first line of gathering stitches, again don't reverse stitch. Just take the fabric out of the machine and cut the threads, leaving long thread ends on the needle and the bobbin.

5 Machine your second row of gathering stitches in between the first row and the edge of the fabric.

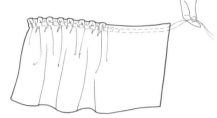

7 At the other end of the gathering stitches, hold onto the two thread ends on the bobbin side and pull, moving the fabric gradually along the rows of stitching. NOTE: the ends of the needle threads should still be on the other side of the fabric.

6 Secure one end only (the same end!) of each row of stitching by pulling the bobbin thread through–pull on the end of the needle thread and a loop should appear around the last stitch. Pull the loop until you find the end of the thread, then knot the two threads together.

8 Continue carefully moving the fabric along until the edge of the gathered fabric has reached a set measurement or is the right size to be attached to another pattern piece, as explained in the project instructions.

9 When the fabric has been gathered to the right length, pull the two needle threads through from the other side of the fabric (that you haven't been pulling on) as described in step 6 and knot all four threads securely.

10 Distribute the gathers evenly.

PLEATS

A pleat is a fold or series of folds in fabric that add fullness into a garment. Pleats can look neater and have a flatter appearance than fullness added by gathers. All pleats are different combinations of the most basic kind of pleat: the knife pleat, which is formed with just two folds going in opposite directions to each other. An inverted pleat is formed from two knife pleats going in opposite directions and positioned side by side.

HOW TO SEW INVERTED PLEATS

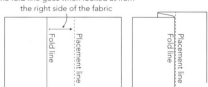

This arrow tells you in which direction the fold line goes when looked at from the right side of the fabric

1 Accurately transfer the fold and placement lines of your pleat from your paper pattern onto the wrong side of your fabric (see Fabrics–Transferring Pattern Markings, page 133). All pleats are shown with these two lines and an arrow showing you in which direction the fold line should lay when looked at from the right side of the fabric.

2 Once you've marked the pleat on your fabric, bring the two lines together, with the right side of the fabric touching, and pin and baste (tack) for approx. 2 in. (5 cm) down these lines. (For the pleats in the Rusholme A-line Skirt and Roehampton Culottes, baste the full length of the marked lines.)

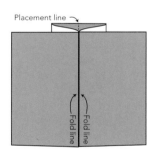

Placement line

3 Flatten the tuck that has been created in the fabric so that it lies against the rest of the garment, with the basted-together fold lines level with the placement line. Press carefully in this position.

4 With the pleat pressed and pinned in place, baste a square around the top of the pleat to keep it in the right position while the rest of the garment is being assembled.

5 All the basting stitches in pleats can be removed once your garment is complete and before you sew the hem.

TIP

If a garment has lots of pleats (like the pleated hem version of the Finsbury Bubble Skirt), I recommend marking all the fold and placement lines with lines of basting (tacking) stitches in a contrasting color, as you can quickly get confused as to which gaps are pleats and which aren't. If you only have a few (like the pleated versions of the Rusholme A-line Skirt or Roehampton Culottes), you can just mark the lines with chalk on the wrong side of the fabric.

POCKETS

Who doesn't love a skirt with a pocket? Of course, not every style of skirt suits a pocket, so in each of the projects in this book, if that skirt will suit a pocket, I have included a pocket variation for you to try. The most common types of pocket are explained in detail here—a simple in-seam pocket and a front hip/cut-away pocket. The Granville Wrap Skirt (page 16) has the option of a lined patch pocket, but all the instructions for that particular pocket are covered in the project instructions.

IN-SEAM POCKETS

In-seam or side-seam pockets are the easiest pockets to add to a garment and can be very inconspicuous as they simply look like an opening in the side seam. I have designed my in-seam pocket bags to be caught in the waistband of the skirt as well as just the side seam. I find that this helps to prevent the skirt from being pulled out of shape by the pocket and provides extra support for the pocket when it's used.

In-seam pockets work best in garments that have some fullness over the hips and can be used in the following projects: Hollings Circle Skirt, Finsbury Bubble Skirt, and Brighton Front-opening Skirt.

TIP

For lighter-weight fabrics that may stretch or wear easily, apply a strip of interfacing to the wrong side of the fabric along the side-seam edges of the front and back skirt pieces between the dots marking the pocket opening and extending ³⁄₈ in. (1 cm) beyond each dot. Use a lightweight iron-on interfacing, cut the strip ¾ in. (2 cm) wide, and place one of the long edges a fraction inside the edge of the fabric.

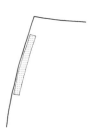

1 For each pocket you will need two pocket bags (a pair rather than two identical ones)—so, for a pocket on each side seam, cut four pocket bags (two pairs).

2 Zig-zag the curved edges of the pocket bags.

4 Pin, baste (tack), and straight stitch along the full length of the side seam edge of the pocket bag, using only a ³⁄₈-in. (1-cm) seam allowance. Repeat with the other pocket bag and the other side seam of the skirt front, then do the same with the skirt back.

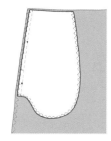

5 Neaten the full length of all four side-seam edges of the skirt front and back, including the edges of the pocket bags.

3 With right sides together, place one pocket bag on the corresponding side seam of the skirt front. Make sure you match up the dots that mark the pocket opening and the notch at the hip along the side-seam edges of the pocket bag and the skirt.

6 Press the pocket bags away from the skirt, so that they stick out like ears!

7 Underststitch the seam (see Seams–Understitching, page 138).

8 When you reach the stage of joining the side seams in your project, place the front and back of the skirt right sides together, with the pocket bags still sticking out to the sides. Pin and machine the side seams from the waist, using a ⅝-in. (1.5-cm) seam allowance. Stop when you are level with the first dot at the top of the pocket opening, reverse stitch, and remove the fabric from your machine.

9 Repeat step 8, starting at the lower dot and continuing to the skirt hem, pinning first and using a ⅝-in. (1.5-cm) seam allowance.

10 Start again at the top waist edge of the outer curve of the pocket bags, pinning them together. Machine with a ⅝-in. (1.5-cm) seam allowance, following the curve of the pocket bag and stopping at the side seam.

11 To press the side seams open: at the lower edge of each pocket, where the pockets meet the side seams, snip into the seam allowance of the back only. The pocket is now able to hang toward the front of your skirt.

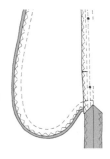

12 Continue to put together the rest of your garment as described in the project instructions.

TIP
To make a feature of your side-seam pockets you could topstitch them to the front of your garment.

FRONT HIP OR CUT-AWAY POCKETS

This is the style of pocket you find on the front of traditional-style five-pocket jeans. They work well in most styles of garment and lend themselves to much more variation than the simple in-seam pocket. The facing part of the pocket can be made in a contrast fabric and the pocket openings can be different shapes.

These pockets can be used in the following projects: Rusholme A-line Skirt and Roehampton Culottes.

1 With right sides together, matching the pocket opening dots, pin each top pocket bag onto each curved pocket opening edge of the skirt front. Machine in place and clip the curves (see Seams–Neatening Seam Allowances, page 137).

2 Press the seams toward the pocket bags and understitch (see Seams–Understitching, page 138).

3 Lay the skirt front wrong side up, then fold the top pocket bags over along the previous seam line, so that the front and pocket bags are wrong sides together.

4 With right sides together, matching the dots and hip notch, pin each front facing and under pocket bag onto each top pocket bag. Machine the two layers together around the curved edges only, and zig-zag the seam allowances together.

5 Baste (tack) the pocket in position across the waist and side-seam edges.

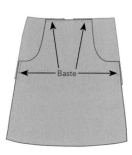

6 Continue to put together the rest of your garment as described in the project instructions.

FITTING

Few of us are standard size-chart proportions, so I'm going to show you how to identify if you will need to alter a pattern and then where and how to alter it.

All the skirts in this book are designed to sit on the natural waistline—I find that skirts that sit here are more comfortable. This tends to be the narrowest part of the body and so is where the waist of a garment naturally wants to settle. However, if you aren't used to wearing things on your natural waist, I will also show you how to lower the waist of the skirts.

DO YOU NEED TO ADJUST THE SIZE OF THE PATTERN?

The sizing system used for the projects is based on actual body measurements of the hip–i.e. a size 41 in. (104 cm) is designed to fit someone with a hip measurement of 41 in. (104 cm) and a waist measurement of 31½ in. (80 cm).

Choose your size based on your hip measurement for these projects: Rusholme A-line Skirt, Roehampton Culottes, Fallowfield Pencil Skirt, Granville Wrap Skirt, Roewood Jersey Pencil Skirt, Finsbury Bubble Skirt.

If your waist measurement differs from that given for your chosen hip measurement in the size chart, you will need to tweak the size of the waist of the pattern.

For these projects, choose your size based on your waist measurement, not your hip measurement: The simple gathered version of the Finsbury Bubble Skirt, Brighton Front-opening Skirt.

If your hip measurement differs from the one given for your chosen waist measurement, don't worry as these skirt designs are full and very loose fitting over the hips.

HOW TO ADJUST THE WAIST MEASUREMENT

If you are between sizes, I recommend going up and choosing the bigger size. You can always take in seams to get a better fit. Try your garment on for size as soon as possible in the making process (before attaching waistbands).

The easiest way to adjust the waist for a given hip size is to grade between sizes.

For example, for someone with a hip measurement of 43 in. (109 cm) and a waist measurement of 31½ in. (80 cm), the hip measurement is size 43 in. (109 cm) on the size chart, but the waist measurement matches that for the next size down–size 41 in. (104 cm).

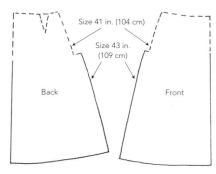
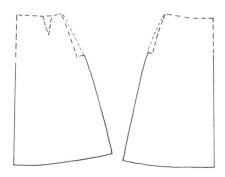

1 Start by tracing the front and back skirt pattern in the size closest to your hip measurement (in this example, 43 in./109 cm). Trace each pattern piece from the hem to the hip level (if the hip level isn't marked with a line on the pattern, it will be marked with a notch on the side seam). Above the hip, trace the size for your waist measurement (in the example given, 41 in./104 cm) and remember to trace any darts to the size that matches your waist measurement.

2 Gradually blend the side seam lines in or out between the hip line and the waist line to create a smooth curve.

3 Trace the waistband or waist facings in the size that matches your waist.

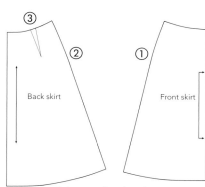

3 places to adjust the waist:
2 side seams (1 and 2) and 1 dart (3)
Multiply by 2 for the whole skirt =
6 places to adjust

I recommend using the grading method for just one size difference. If you need to adjust the waist by more than that (for example, for someone with a hip measurement of 43 in./109 cm and a waist measurement of 30 in./77 cm, the waist measurement is two sizes smaller), grade down one size between hip and waist as previously described and then tweak the waist to fit by spreading the remaining adjustment between the darts and/or the side seams. Fit adjustments work best if they are spread evenly around the garment rather than being concentrated in one place.

1 Work out how much extra you need to adjust the waist by after you have graded between sizes. In the example given, this is 1½ in. (3 cm): we have already graded down one size to a 31½ in. (80 cm) waist, but the actual waist is 30 in. (77 cm).

2 Looking at your front and back skirt pattern pieces, work out how many places are available over which to spread this adjustment–for example, front side seam, back side seam, and any darts. Remember to double the number to include the whole skirt, as each pattern piece is a half pattern representing, respectively, half the back skirt and half the front skirt.

3 Divide the amount you need to adjust by the number of places you have available to make the adjustment: e.g. 1½ in. (3 cm) divided by 6 (4 side seam edges and 2 darts) = ¼ in. (0.5 cm) at each adjustment point.

4 You can safely make a total adjustment of up to 1½ in. (4 cm) to the side seams only. If you need to adjust by more than this, you will need to spread it across the darts, too.

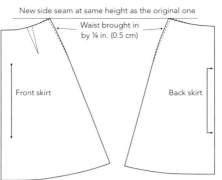

New side seam at same height as the original one

Waist brought in by ¼ in. (0.5 cm)

Front skirt

Back skirt

Total amount adjusted = 1 in. (2 cm)

5 To adjust at the side seams
Bring the waist edge of each side seam in by ¼ in. (0.5 cm), tapering back into the original side seam at hip level, keeping the top of the new side seam at the same height as the original one. (To increase the waist size, draw the new line outside the original side-seam line.)

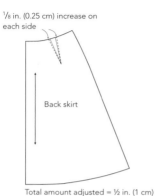

⅛ in. (0.25 cm) increase on each side

Back skirt

Total amount adjusted = ½ in. (1 cm)

6 To adjust at the darts
Increase each side of the dart by ⅛ in. (0.25 cm). There is one dart on each back piece, so the total adjustment is ½ in. (1 cm). (To increase the waist size, decrease the size of the dart.)

7 Remember to adjust your waistband or waist facings by the same amount. Waistbands can simply have the adjustment added or removed from one end; waist facings need to be adjusted at the side seams.

If you also need to make minor width adjustments at the hips, do it at the side seams only and be sure to add on or take off the same amount in the same place on the front and back pattern pieces. This is probably best determined when you try the skirt on for the first time.

HOW TO LOWER THE WAIST

If you don't want to wear your skirt on your natural waistline the easiest way to work out how much to lower the waist is by using an existing garment that sits in the right place.

1 Tie a piece of string around your natural waist (see Sizing & Taking Measurements, page 130).

2 Put on an existing garment that sits in your preferred place.

3 Measure the distance between the string and the top edge of the garment at the front of your body (don't try to measure it at the side, as you will lean over which will change the measurement).

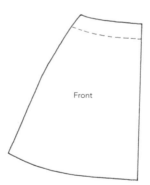

Front

4 Once you know how much you want to lower the waist by, mark that distance at regular intervals from the top waist edge of the front and back skirt pattern pieces.

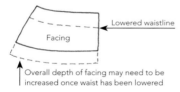

Lowered waistline

Facing

Overall depth of facing may need to be increased once waist has been lowered

5 If your chosen skirt is finished with a waist facing, you will need to do the same thing to the front and back waist facing pattern pieces. You may then also need increase the depth of the facing at the bottom edge. I find few things in garments more irritating than shallow flappy facings.

6 If your chosen skirt is finished with a waistband, measure the original waistline of the skirt (less seam allowances, then double the measurement as you are working with half a pattern). Compare this with the measurement of the waist at your new lowered position, then add the difference between the two measurements to your waistband. Add it to the end without the underwrap and re-mark the seam allowance notch at the end–but be aware that all your other notches and dots marking side seams and centers will be out.

FABRIC GLOSSARY

I have separated this glossary into two sections: a list of the common fibers used to make fabrics, along with their key properties, and a list of the most commonly used fabrics, along with useful descriptions of what garments and styles they suit. I hope that this will not only help you in your fabric selections, but also help you to better understand fabrics in general.

First, to be successful in choosing the right fabric for your project, you must understand the difference between fibers and fabrics. Fiber is the raw material (such as cotton or polyester) that is spun into a yarn. Fabric is the cloth that is made by weaving or knitting yarns together. The best way to explain the difference is with an example: cotton jersey and viscose jersey are the same "type" of fabric (jersey), but made from different fibers (one cotton, one viscose). As you start to make your own clothes, it is important to start to learn about the properties of different fibers so that you can start to choose the most appropriate fabrics for what you're making.

A helpful note about static fabrics (don't you just hate it when clothes start to stick to you and skirt linings walk up your legs?!): as a general rule, to avoid static electricity build-up in your clothes choose absorbent fibers (especially for linings); the more absorbent a fiber is, the less static it will become.

FIBERS

Bamboo A natural fiber made from bamboo plants, bamboo makes a fabric that feels and behaves a lot like cotton, and is soft and absorbent. It has a reputation as a sustainable natural fiber, as most bamboo fiber is organic and it needs much less water than cotton to grow. Can be machine washed and dried.

Cotton A natural fiber from the cotton plant, it is absorbent but can take a long time to dry. Cotton creases, but is soft and strong, which makes it popular for clothing worn next to the skin as well as for clothes that need to withstand some wear and tear. Organic cotton is becoming much more widely available and is a preferable choice over conventional cotton. Can be machine washed and dried.

Cupro Sometimes called man-made silk, cupro is a regenerated fiber made from cotton linter (very fine silky fibers left over after traditional cotton production). Cupro retains the breathability of cotton and is not static, making it a good choice for lining fabrics. Also known as Bemberg, a brand name for cupro fiber. It is often chosen by vegans who object to the way that conventional silk is produced. Can be machine washed and dried.

Elastane (known as spandex in the US) An elastic, man-made fiber that is often mixed with other fibers to make stretch fabrics. The higher the elastane content in your fabric, the stretchier it will be. Also known as Lycra, although this is a brand name for DuPont's elastane fiber. Can be machine washed and dried at a low heat.

Linen Another natural fiber, linen comes from the flax plant. The main quality of linen that most people recognize is its tendency to crease! However, it's worth noting that the higher the thread count (the density of yarns per square inch of fabric) of a linen fabric, the less it will crease. It is also absorbent and dries quickly, making it cool to wear. Linen is stronger than cotton, so it is good for garments that are subject to some wear and tear; think of all those farmers' smocks from the 1800s. Linen fabrics become softer with repeated wearing. Can be machine washed and dried.

Modal A type of rayon made from wood pulp–usually from beech trees–Modal is a brand name for this particular type of rayon. It looks and feels like a very smooth soft cotton, is very absorbent, and is often mixed with cotton. Can be machine washed and dried at a low heat.

Nylon A man-made fiber that originates from oil. It is strong, can be wind- and water resistant, and dries quickly, making it popular for use in outdoor and sports clothing and accessories. As it is sensitive to heat, it must be washed and ironed on a low temperature. It isn't absorbent and so can be uncomfortable to wear in heat.

Polyester Another man-made fiber originating from oil. It is strong and water resistant, so dries quickly. Because polyester is crease resistant, it is often blended with other fibers such as cotton. It isn't absorbent and so can be uncomfortable to wear in heat–something to bear in mind if you see it in a mixed-fiber fabric. Can be machine washed and dried on a low heat.

Rayon Similar to cupro and viscose, rayon is a regenerated fiber made from wood pulp. It can be made to mimic most natural fibers, commonly silk, cotton, and linen. It is smooth with good drape, and very absorbent, but doesn't dry quickly. It must be washed at lower temperatures and is often labeled "dry clean only."

Silk The strongest natural fiber, made from the cocoon of the silk worm. The fibers are extremely long, making it a lustrous fiber that creates very drapey fabrics. Silk fabrics are susceptible to moths, especially if stored unclean. Silk is absorbent but dries quickly, making it comfortable to wear next to the skin, although this can also make it susceptible to becoming static. Silk is best washed very gently by hand with a specialist gentle detergent with minimum agitation; don't soak silk and don't leave it damp, creased, and crumpled. Do not tumble dry! Silk is best hung to dry.

Tencel Like Modal, Tencel is another type of rayon made from wood pulp, this one from the eucalyptus tree. Tencel is a brand name; the fabric is also known as lyocell. As with rayon, Tencel can be made to resemble silk, cotton, and linen, and is often blended with these fibers. It is very absorbent, with great drape. It is claimed that Tencel is the most sustainable of this regenerated group of fibers, as the eucalyptus trees from which it is made are grown sustainably. Again it is best washed at lower temperatures.

Viscose Man made, but known as a regenerated fiber as it is made from wood pulp (typically soy, bamboo, or sugar cane), viscose is a type of rayon, but made in a slightly different way. It has a beautiful heavy drape and is absorbent, making it more comfortable to wear than nylon or polyester. It can take a long time to dry, though, and is often prone to creasing. It is best washed at lower temperatures.

Wool A natural fiber from the fleece of animals such as sheep, goats, and even rabbits (includes alpaca, angora, and mohair), wool can be made into a wide range of fabrics and is naturally warm to wear. Although it is not absorbent, moisture can pass through its structure making it comfortable to wear; it is naturally breathable. Wool doesn't need much ironing and is flame retardant. Wool fabrics have a bit of natural "give" or elasticity, making them easy to manipulate. Prone to shrinking and pilling, both of which are natural processes for wool, it needs to be handled carefully. Some wool fabrics are machine washable; check the label. If not, hand wash with a specialist gentle detergent and minimum agitation. Don't tumble dry wool; it's best dried flat.

FABRICS

Calico A plain, woven fabric in cotton, usually unbleached. Useful for making toiles or sample/prototype garments.

Canvas A plain, woven (sometimes twill), medium or heavy in weight, usually in cotton. Good for hardwearing, structured garments. Also known as "duck" or "sailcloth."

Challis A lightweight, soft, woven fabric, usually made from cotton, silk, wool, or rayon. Great for gathered, floaty, and draped styles.

Chambray A plain, woven fabric that looks like a light shirting-weight version of denim. Usually cotton and woven from fine threads, with a colored thread on the warp and white on the weft giving the denim look. Great for shirts and crisp but lightweight garments and will hold pleats well.

Charmeuse A lightweight, woven fabric with a satin weave on the right side to create a smooth sheen (the wrong side is matt). Usually made from silk or polyester, it's great for gathered, floaty, and draped styles. Not to be confused with crepe back satin, which looks similar (with a shiny and a matt side) but is heavier.

Chintz A medium-weight, plain, woven cotton fabric with a glazed finish to give the surface a sheen; a crisp fabric that will hold its shape well.

Corduroy A woven fabric, usually from cotton with a fluffy surface texture (called a pile or nap–see Velvet), which is woven and cut into ridges, creating vertical lines down the fabric. Warm and fairly hardwearing, it's good for structured garments and will hold details such as pockets well.

Crepe A lightweight woven fabric with a slightly textured, wrinkled surface. Usually in silk, viscose, or polyester, it has a lovely drapey hang that is comfortable to wear and is great for full, draped styles.

Denim A woven fabric, usually in cotton, with a colored warp thread (usually blue) and a white weft giving the distinct coloring. Strong and hardwearing, it's usually medium- to heavy weight and gives a characteristic "utility" or "workwear" feel to any garment it's used in. If a colored warp thread isn't used, the plain colored fabric is known as "drill."

Dupion Always silk, dupion (also known as dupioni) is a plain, woven silk that has a very crisp texture, sometimes almost paper-like. It's very lightweight to wear and the surface has a slubby, uneven texture. It looks identical on both sides of the fabric and has a lovely sheen. It's great for very structured, voluminous styles and will hold details like pleats well.

French terry Typically known as sweatshirt fabric, often in cotton, but sometimes polyester/cotton blends. A knitted fabric that can be medium- to heavy in weight, the right side is flat and smooth and looks like a plain knitted fabric, while the back has a texture made up of loops of threads (which can look like terry toweling). This construction makes it comfortable to wear, as the cotton is absorbent, but the textured wrong side can trap heat. The loops on the wrong side can also be brushed, making it soft against the skin. Hardwearing, it's mostly used for casual and sports clothing.

Interlock A knitted fabric that looks the same on the right and wrong side. Usually in cotton, it is a bit heavier than jersey and is soft and comfortable to wear. Good for fitted styles.

Jersey The most basic and common knitted fabric. Can be single jersey or slightly thicker double jersey commonly cotton, wool, or silk, often combined with elastane. Great for fitted body-con styles.

Lawn A woven fabric, usually in cotton but can also be linen, lawn uses very fine threads and is densely woven, which gives it a crisp lightweight finish. A good alternative for linings if you don't like smooth, shiny, lining fabrics.

Muslin A very lightweight, woven fabric with an open weave, cotton muslin is preferable to poly/cotton, especially if you use it for making pressing cloths.

Needlecord A lighter-weight, softer, fine version of corduroy. Not as hardwearing or warm, and as it's a bit more floppy than corduroy, it won't hold its shape as well.

Noil A medium-weight, woven fabric made from the fibers left over from silk spinning, noil has a a slubby, uneven textured surface. It is also known as "raw silk."

Ponte Roma Sometimes called Ponte di Roma, or just ponti or ponte, or roma. Ponte di Roma means "Roman Bridge," which describes the texture on the surface of the fabric. Another type of double-knit interlock fabric, it is usually quite thick and heavy and so can be used for more structured dresses and jackets. Often made from synthetic fibers such as polyester, the best-quality Ponte Roma is viscose. It also usually contains elastane.

Poplin A light- to medium-weight plain but fairly densely woven fabric, with a matt surface on both the right and wrong sides. Crisp and holds its shape well. Commonly made from cotton or polyester/cotton blends, but also from silk, wool, rayon, or viscose.

Quilting cotton A plain, woven, medium-weight cotton fabric, often with a bright or novelty print, usually narrow in width. Intended for use in patchwork and quilting, it can be used in dressmaking, but can be quite stiff, so it doesn't drape well and is best for structured, simple styles.

Satin Describes the type of weave used in the fabric. The weft threads tend to be a light, lustruous fiber, which results in a lightweight fabric that has a sheen to the right side, with a dull wrong side and a lovely drape. Usually made from silk or polyester. Good for loose, gathered, and draped styles.

Sateen A woven fabric, usually in cotton. The way that the threads are woven results in a smooth, soft fabric with a very subtle sheen to the surface. A bit heavier than satin, sateen is great for structured and fitted styles, especially with the addition of elastane.

Sweatshirt See French terry.

Taffeta A very crisp, plain, and densely woven light- to medium-weight fabric, with a smooth surface with a sheen that looks the same on both the right and the wrong side. It has a distinctive rustle due to its crisp nature and creases easily. Usually made from silk but can be cupro or rayon. Great for structured, voluminous styles, taffeta has very little drape so will appear quite stiff.

Tweed A woven wool fabric with quite a rough feel, often with brightly colored flecks. Good for structured styles, but needs lining for comfort.

Velvet A medium- to heavy weight woven fabric with a textured surface on the right side. The textured surface is formed from tufts in the weave that are then cut to form a "pile." This surface can also be described as being "napped" and the pattern pieces must all be cut in the same direction. Often made from cotton and sometimes silk. Viscose or rayon are often used as cheaper substitutes for silk. Velvet is best for simple, structured shapes with minimal seams and details. It is warm to wear.

SUPPLIERS

Most of the beautiful fabrics used in the book were purchased from Gill Thornley at Ditto Fabrics in Brighton–thanks for letting me have first dibs, Gill!

The neon pink feather print wrap skirt and the black-and-white print front-opening skirt were from Fiona Trevaskiss at Faberwood–thanks for all your support, Fiona, and for having such a good eye for selecting beautiful fabrics.

The distinctive multi-colored fabric used in the pencil skirt with the back vent was hand dyed for me by Ce Persiano of The Uncommon Thread. Thanks for creating the most beautiful piece of fabric, Ce, and I'm looking forward to more playing with paint and dye! All the buttons were from Maggie at Textile Garden who sources the most beautiful-quality buttons you will ever see.

US SUPPLIERS

Fabric Depot
www.fabricdepot.com

Fabricland
www.fabricland.com

Hobby Lobby
www.hobbylobby.com

Joann Fabrics and Craft Stores
www.joann.com

Michaels
www.michaels.com

UK SUPPLIERS

The Cloth House
www.clothhouse.com

Ditto Fabrics
www.dittofabrics.co.uk

Faberwood Fabrics
www.faberwood.com

Hobbycraft
www.hobbycraft.co.uk

John Lewis
www.johnlewis.co.uk

INDEX

ACKNOWLEDGMENTS

It takes an amazing team to create wonderful things and this book is the result of a shared vision and huge amount of work.

Thanks first to a wonderful team at CICO Books; Cindy Richards for believing in me and my idea and commissioning the book, Anna Galkina for being quite simply wonderful in supporting and encouraging my progress and sharing my vision, Sally Powell for being on my creative wavelength, Sarah Hoggett for being a super eagle-eyed editor who always had a solution for any problems we came up against, and the enthusiastic publicity and marketing team of Yvonne Doolan, Polly Grice, and Jen Hampson.

It was a joy to be able to work with photographer Julian Ward again on this book; it's always a pleasure to work with someone who instinctively understands what you're trying to do and is so technically and creatively brilliant that they can just make it happen.

Rob Merrett, you are a creative force of nature! Thank you for sharing your years of experience, for your creative eye, and for being able to style an outfit in ways that wouldn't even have occurred to me; you took me just the right side of girly! Not to mention for making me laugh so much.

All my eager students at MIY Workshop deserve a big thanks for keeping me on my toes and ensuring I never stop learning.

And last but never least, Patrick for endless cooking and washing-up and for always being there through the lows as well as the highs.